INSTA-PRAISE FROM ~~BOOKSTAGR~~AMMERS

"It has been s̶o̶ ... ̶ heart has been truly touched. I am ... ̶ give *Lost in Beirut* justice. I fall asleep thinking ̶ ... ̶nd it's been on my mind every day. I loved every second of this book: I simply did not want it to end, so much that I had to pace myself. I have always believed that it isn't right to give a star rating to true stories, but you just can't deny the fact that this book deserves infinite stars. Such a beautifully written book! Every second of it felt like a rollercoaster- from moments that made me laugh to moments that made me cry. Everyone needs to read this book at least once in their lifetime, I can't emphasize it enough! *Lost in Beirut*, my favorite read of the year thus far!"

—*Celina | @moonoverbooks*

"WOW... this book is definitely the dark horse of the year! I have to be honest; I did not expect to like this book much less connect to it. *LIB* is a nonfiction showstopper that will have you thinking 'there is no way this happened.' The story isn't just about war - it is full of love, loss, and so much faith that I could not put it down. It's also about being true to yourself and being present in the moment because tomorrow is never promised. Quick, fast-paced read, that had me on edge. The writing is excellent- the whole time it was like watching a movie. I could feel Ashe's emotions through his experience. The ending chapter in the Paris airport was so beautiful. This story will stick with me for a while."

—*Christy deClairmont | @readwithchristy*

"A very moving story that tugs at you while you read about how powerful love, loss and war can truly be. There were intriguing aspects of this story, from the lifestyle that felt so elite to being trapped in a foreign country at war. The way faith and hope are woven together creates such a weighty addition to the story. Captivating storytelling you can't help but feel like, wow I can't believe this is real. Some parts so heartbreaking to read, my heart ached long after finishing. This story is going to stick with me."

—*Babs | @babs_reviews*

"It is a divine awakening, an inspiration to a wandering soul. It sets a question of purpose, the unforeseen journey, and the immeasurable answers to one's longings. It's the second book I've read this year that gave me that 'cannot move on' feeling. I refused to read other books days after *LIB* and took my time to be consumed with the emotions I had during the reading process. It will move you in ways you cannot imagine. *Lost in Beirut* is an account of life's uncertainties and vulnerabilities strongly shared with readers, a gem to behold."

—*Carmen* | *@book.sanity*

"This was one of my most anticipated reads and it did not disappoint! *Lost in Beirut* is a beautiful, true story about love, loss, and tragedy - and it takes place in my home country, Lebanon. I started it on a flight home and absolutely couldn't put it down. Reading about Ashe's experience was so surreal! It was perfectly descriptive and full of emotion, and I felt the heartbreak immensely at the end and it highlighted the reality of a war-torn country and feeling completely lost amidst the chaos. But it also shined a light on the people of Lebanon and how resilient they are. It made me feel so proud to be Lebanese."

—*Malissa* | *@meesreads*

"This true story takes you on such a wild ride it's hard for you to put it down. I felt so many emotions while reading this book, I laughed, I was shocked and was extremely anxious on almost every single page! I loved the culture representation & reading about the upscale vibes of Lebanon. When I finished this book, I remember closing it and saying "WOW"."

—*Naomie* | *@naesreadingnook*

"I have a lingering bittersweet feeling having finished the final chapter. I enjoyed the eloquent writing. While reading it, I could sense each detail as if I was present with Ashe in the moment. The smell, the touch and the images. The war, the fear and desperation for survival. The kisses, the full hearts and the party nights. This book was captivating, it kept me on edge to find answers and crushed yet healed my heart all in one. I'm Lebanese myself and I appreciate the way Lebanon was portrayed, I appreciate the wonderful relationships Ashe built with the Lebanese people and I value the awareness raised in this book."

—*Keely* | *@bookswith_kb*

"*Lost in Beirut* is a book of love, hope and a faith that could move mountains. I truly couldn't put this book down. There were times, I kept thinking to myself that this is insane and I can't believe this is real. I felt like I was watching a movie and right there alongside Ashe the whole time throughout his time leading up to and during the start of the Lebanon War in 2006. I cannot adequately put into words what this book made me feel and I wholeheartedly will recommend this book to anyone."

—*Amber | @ambersbooksandcoffee*

"I could not put this book down. This memoir was quite different than any others that I have read. It was really captivating and almost felt like watching a movie. And the writing is so intense that you are able to feel Ashe's emotions through his experience. It is a reminder that no day is promised and really made me take a step back and evaluate where I am in my life. This memoir definitely is one that will stick out and I cannot recommend it enough."

—*Steph | @paperbackswithsteph*

"You can tell Ashe is a natural born storyteller, his clever, optimistic and insightful voice is clear and consistent. I don't usually mark my books, but there were some particularly poignant and vivid imagery used (for example, at one point, someone is referred to as having a "straw heart"). I thoroughly recommend this book, as it has a little bit of everything; romance, action, comedy and it shares some beautiful life lessons. I have a feeling this is only scratching the surface of stories that they have to tell and I can't wait to read what's next!"

—*Justin Pitt | @just_in_print*

"This memoir feels just like a novel and you'll cry, laugh and devour every single moment with the narrator. The writing style is so important for a reader like me, and this book had a perfect one. It's a heartwarming story of love, loss, war and endurance & how people react in these situations. I urge you all to read this beautiful book."

—*Kashmala | @maalalifechapters*

"Reading *Lost in Beirut* felt like watching a film, I was right there with Ashe as he maneuvered through what was probably his biggest summer of self-discovery. I loved his vibe and how he loved deeply and embraced the love conquers all motto."

—*Sarah Matlock | @bookedupandcaffeinated*

"A memoir isn't something I usually read but I'm so happy I decided to pick this up because this story is so beautiful and tragic and truly something special. From page one until I closed the book at the end, I was pulled in to Ashe's story. At some point I completely forgot I'm reading a memoir. I'm thinking 'omg, this is such a good book!' And then I had to slap myself and remember that this is something someone actually lived through. I feel so many emotions after reading this."

—Kate | @catmomreadsbooks

"What an awe inspiring true story that I was in no way prepared for. This is a story of hope, anguish, love, and war. It is deeply emotional, and enlightening. There were so many things that happened that left my jaw dropped, especially towards the end. Ashe, thank you for sharing your story with us. For being brave enough to live it first, and tell it second. I am inspired by your courage and your compassion."

—Jennalee Hutchinson | @theruggedbookshelf

"For someone that usually struggles with nonfiction, books like this are magical. I was transported to another place and time, and watched this period of time unfold through Ashe's eyes. I loved the friendship between Danny and Ashe, and I loved that they stuck together during difficult times. The ending had me blinking back tears, mostly out of relief for Ashe, but also because the story culminated beautifully. It teaches you to appreciate every single day, because things can change in the blink of an eye. This is a book everyone should read."

— Chrisell | @abundleofbookss

"This one is unputdownable! I was totally engrossed in this impactful story from start to finish. This story is so beautifully written and Ashe's storytelling is so captivating and mesmerizing. It is a little book that is packed from start to finish with a story of love, loss, hope, and such an important message of faith and never giving up. Even if you are not a fan of memoirs I highly recommend you pick this one up!"

—Melanie G. | @addictedtobooks86

"This memoir captivated me from the beginning. I traveled to Lebanon when I was 18 for 5 weeks and a lot of what Ashe describes really brought me back. The "carpe diem" sentiment he captures so well. To hear Ashe's story from the perspective of an American trapped was really insightful. If you love a good memoir that will take you on a fast pace journey I highly recommend this book. It felt like watching a film and there were so many moments of self-reflection that I really appreciated."

—*Lina | @bookishly_overdue*

"A beautifully written book, with an incredible and eye-opening story. The adventures and experiences Ashe has before the war was so amazing and almost too good to be true, and it was incredibly heartbreaking to read about how one can have everything you need in life, and then lose it almost as fast as blinking an eye. Something that was really interesting about reading this book was the contrasts. Both with Beirut but also Ashe himself. It was interesting to see the challenges Ashe faces both before and after the bombing starts, in terms of him being an American. The writing was beautiful! It is written with a poetic and spiritual style which enhanced the book and its story so much."

—*Carina | @carinasbooks_*

"Raw. Real. Eye-opening. Ashe's journey teaches us lessons on life, love, and sacrifice. This memoir is not like the ordinary. It stood out from the rest. There were so many layers and so much deep rooted meaning in each chapter. I loved how it was told in scuba subjective way. How it tests you in every single way. It tests your faith and your relationships. I am so happy that I was able to come across this memorable book. Furthermore, the amount of love, time and patience that Ashe and Dr. Magdalena Stevens put into writing this novel is evident when you read it."

—*Ash | @eat.pray.decorate*

"This is actually my first memoir and also the first book which made me cry. I devoured this memoir. I couldn't put it down. I was totally hooked! It is wonderfully written and a fast-paced read that provoked a lot of emotions. Such a roller coaster indeed! It feels like I'm watching a movie. I do hope that this book gets a film adaptation one day. "

—*Eve Cerico | @evoreads_*

"This book was amazing and couldn't put it down until I finished it! I was kind of surprised by how much I enjoyed it because I typically go for fiction, but I am so glad to have read this. It was filled with such raw emotion and dealt with love, loss, and a lot of hope and faith. It provided a different perspective on the Lebanon War and I'm grateful to have been given a glimpse of that. There are a lot of moments from this book that I think will stick with me, but there was something so touching about that final chapter in the airport. I feel so inspired after having read this and will always be seeking to "fill my vessel.""

—*Madison | @madsbookstagram*

"The writing was beautiful! This book captured my soul and took me back to a beautiful time in my life, when I first visited the magnificent Beirut. I felt like I was Ashe and I was in Beirut! Not many books have ever made me feel that way. I felt every single page of this book and every single emotion that Ashe and his friends felt. Every happy moment, every beat of music in those Beirut night clubs, and every bit of anxiety during the war. Absolutely amazing writing! The story is so touching! I would recommend this to every reader around the world. This book is full of beauty, love, family, friendship, war and peace!"

—*Nadia Saad | @nadias.bookshelf*

"Wow, this story. I had to take a few days to wrap my head around it. The beginning of the novel makes you feel one way and then Ashe and Magdalena make you feel a whole different set of emotions in the other half. And the way these two wrote and told the story was beautiful. It's filled with so many incredible lines and moments that had I annotated, I think I would have just underlined 90% of the book. I didn't expect for it to hit me the way it did. I think I felt just about every emotion possible."

—*Allyson | @thebookish.mama*

"This book is so beautifully written. I honestly didn't want to finish it because I was so lost in it (pun intended). I don't usually read memoirs but this one really hit differently. I felt every emotion that has been described in the book deeply. The message of the book is that tomorrow is not promised, so treasure every moment and live like there is no tomorrow, and I absolutely loved that. I will forever treasure this book. The writing is exquisite and the fact that it's a true story is just *chefs kiss*."

— *Shams Sapte | @readwshams*

"Wow - this book was quite the rollercoaster! I loved learning more about the culture and the Lebanon War in 2006. With wonderfully written descriptions, this was a fast paced story that provoked a lot of emotions right up to the ending! The story this book tells is an important one full of mystery, love, and hope. It really made me reflect on my life living in the USA. This story is definitely going to stick with me, and I will treasure the time I have spent reading it!"

—*Emma March | @anneofreadgables*

"Wow! This is a 5-star read all the way. It's a page turner, fast paced, and a hard to put down book. Never a dull page. The writing is beautiful and speaks to the reader profoundly. I loved the metaphors in this book. My soul was out in Lebanon partying. Jamming out to 50 Cent! I laughed, cried, and I held my kid tight. And I'll keep it at that. Just like the cover, you're gonna have to dive in this adventure."

— *Lisset | @lisb.bookshelfies*

"I'm sitting here writing this review in my air conditioned home that *Lost in Beirut* has made me eternally grateful for. If I could sum up Ashe's story in one word, it would be: impactful. After a few days and my thoughts have really had a chance to settle, I realize that this memoir is truly one of the best I've ever read and probably will ever read. *Lost in Beirut* was the beautiful eye-opener I didn't know I needed. This book follows Ashe Stevens as he transforms from an American party boy/actor into a true 'world citizen'. My biggest takeaways are the strength of the human spirit and people's capacity to love. No matter whether you love romance, thrillers, historical novels etc. - there aren't many people who wouldn't love this one!"

— *@southern.lady.reads*

LOST IN BEIRUT

LOST IN BEIRUT

A True Story of Love, Loss and War

Ashe & Magdalena Stevens

Published by Anounymous Inc.

lostinbeirut.com
Cover design by COVERKITCHEN

The cataloging-in-publication data is on file
at the Library of Congress
LCCN: 2021920857
ISBN: 978-1-7379524-7-3

First Edition Published 2021

For you...

DESERT WHISPERS

"Life teaches me that anything not growing is dead."

AUGUST 9TH, 2006, AMMAN CIVIL AIRPORT, JORDAN. The sun is as hot as I thought it would be in the desert. I often thought about how Jesus wandered in the Jordanian desert for 40 days and 40 nights, and he survived. Now I know. The Bedouin taught me not to travel during the day. They set up camp and sleep in the day and walk the desert in the cool air of starry nights. There is something about the wind in the desert. It carries memories. Surrounded by people shouting in Arabic gives me the sensation of hearing people talk in English. Maybe it's just my loved ones coming back to me in the whispers of the desert. I am sitting here beaten, hungry, lost. The new hole in my belt is evidence of the weight I have lost in the past few weeks. If I could scream, I would, but they have reprimanded me for speaking, out of the fear of drawing attention to myself. In this land, being an American can get you kidnapped, ransomed or possibly beheaded online for the world to see.

This desert heat has caused such severe dehydration that I can scarcely think straight. My brain must not be getting enough oxygen because I have trouble discerning reality from hallucination. I see her everywhere, but she is nowhere. Catching a glimpse of her, I reach out to touch her, but she fades into the heat-simmering light.

I don't know if I will see her one last time, or am I just waiting for death to pick me up here? Death is busy in this land; thousands have lost their lives. Only we, the refugees, stranded for days at this airport, are the witnesses to the political lies of when this will stop. I miss the comfort, the security, the feeling of freedom and safety I took for granted as an American. Not sure if it's a sign, but somehow through the nauseating stench of the airport, I can almost smell the desert pine trees in the courtyard of the California Institute of the Arts. If I just close my eyes and concentrate hard enough, I can escape and imagine myself, almost a decade ago, running through the tiled green halls, late for mask class with the great Rodger Henderson.

THE MASKED VESSEL

"Didn't know I was wearing a mask until he taught me
to look inward."

They look like fingers coming out of the ground, waiting to catch ideas, the same way the Native Americans use dream catchers to enhance visions. I can understand how Tim Burton was inspired by these pine trees. The fresh, calming scent of desert pine always clears my head of worldly distractions as I run into the CalArts main building. Late, I am always late. Running so fast, my sneakers squeak on the tiled floor as I try to cut corners on the staircase. Theater, E106. *Will it open? Or is it locked already?* I turn the knob. *Shit, it's locked! I must knock. He's going to be so mad.* I knock and hear the footsteps get closer as the door opens. He stands there, waving me in like an uninvited guest, the living Jack Skellington. If there was ever a man made for the theater, it is Rodger Henderson. His presence demands your attention. Even in a sea of people on stage, he commands the spotlight. He is a well-known and well-loved Californian stage director, actor and teacher who as a young man found refuge in theater during the Vietnam War and directed productions all around the world, from San Francisco and Sydney to London and Rome. He also happens to be my favorite professor, but I'm biased because he auditioned me for this school, one of the 19 candidates out of about a thousand. His approval is the reason I'm here.

"Now that we're all here," Mr. Henderson says abruptly as he closes the door behind me, "grab your partner and let's continue the mirror exercise."

I'm grateful he has let me in. He can be prickly and usually never does this for anybody. Being late for his class means not only being locked out, but you're expected to wait until he sees you waiting by the door at the end of the class. I quickly take off my clothes and grab my robe and the mask from the costume closet. I can't apologize for my tardiness because we cannot speak or behave as our "normal" selves in this course. As I put on my mask, I remember the countless hours of molding it by hand and all the emotions that went into creating this abstract figure I am about to become.

My partner today is Kirk. As we stand at the corner of the class looking at each other, Rodger's voice inflames our minds: "Who is this person in front of you? It is not the person you have known for the past year. It is someone new. Do you know this person's name? No! You do not! Is this person a friend or an enemy? Do you want to fuck this person, or do you want to kill this person?"

Rodger has a way of tearing down prejudices, whether you are ready or not. *Swim, child, swim... or drown, it's your choice.*

Kirk doesn't even blink beneath the mask. This is not funny. It is an intense deep exploration into us and the character development.

Rodger continues his assault on our presumptions: "Notice! This person in front of you doesn't even walk the same as your friend. Notice, this person doesn't even breathe the same. What are your beliefs? Do you believe in God? Which one? Or just maybe you're so hungry, so starving, you're thinking of eating the person in front of you..."

As my stomach grumbles, my appetite dissipates.

"Or maybe," Rodger's voice lightens, "you would give your life for this person, the ultimate act of love for a stranger or family member. What drives you? Back to beliefs... what do you believe?" His voice rises, "Are you a person of faith? Answer these questions! Goddamn it!!! You MUST know these answers! That is your job as an actor! Now move. Do not walk. You do not know if you can walk. So, you crawl like babies. Craaaaaawl! Look, look at this worm!" he screams as he points to me, covered in dust from crawling all over this dirty black floor. "Is this the only worm in my class, 'cause all I see are birds. I did not grant you permission to fly yet. If you want to fly and not give yourself over to this craft, then fly away. The door will open for you. If you want to be an artist, be here!" He continues to point down to me on the floor.

"Listen! Do not speak or cry. You don't know what your voice sounds like yet. Speaking and walking are the ultimate steps in this course. Keep listening, keep exploring. Open your mind. You have all semester with me."

This assault on our senses continues for the next hour. I'm physically and mentally drained, like everyone in this space. The sweat beneath the mask collects on my chin.

Class is finally over for the day. As I am changing back into my clothes, they feel foreign to me. Why I would wear these clothes escapes my mind. I have keys in my pocket, but it takes me minutes to remember what they're for. Even the steps I make toward the exit feel contrived, foreign to my muscles. We all look the same, leaving this phantom zone. Lost in our own bodies.

Rodger waves at me to stay. I hesitantly make my way over to him. As he sits in his lotus pose on the floor, he gestures at me to sit in front of him. He stares at me, saying nothing.

The silence gets to me after several minutes. "I'm sorry for being late," I blurt out, "and disturbing the sanctity of the space you create for us."

"*Nosce te ipsum*... Ashe," Rodger whispers. *Know thyself.*

This has never happened before, but still it's weird, so I don't say anything.

"Life is so short... do what you can while you can," he goes on. "I see so much promise in you, and that's why you're here. But I fear what I must tell you goes against everything we have taught you in our society. I can get in a lot of trouble for what I'm about to tell you." His face suddenly looks serious.

"I'm present and your words are safe with me," I reply.

Rodger leans in like he's about to share a secret. "Death is knocking at my door, so I don't give a fuck about consequences. I only care about telling you the truth."

As someone who's been battling cancer for over a decade and whose partner had died years before, he is only too aware of the fragility of life. But I am confused about why he's confiding in me.

"This is the last semester I'm teaching this course. I'm going to tell you something that I've told no student in over 20 years of teaching." He lowers his voice, nearly whispering. "After two years of being here, there's nothing more between these hallways that we can teach you, Ashe. Sure, we can show you a little technique, where the commas and exclamation points are. Maybe you will have a little more structure to your craft, but you must find your own story." He points to the mirror.

I sit, shocked, trying to grasp what this teacher, who I always viewed as a sort of father figure, is trying to tell me.

"Look in the mirror. What do you see? Be honest with yourself, what do you see?"

"I see a lost clown without a circus." I say the first thing that comes to mind and, quite unexpectedly, my eyes mist.

"What have you seen? Where have you been? I'll tell you where... you've been tucked away under America's protective blanket. Notre Dame High School, a private school, CalArts, another private school, dinner on the table every night, a good roof over your head. Sure, you may know pain of some sort, but do you have any real empathy? You have only seen one side of the coin of life."

I am speechless, taking in the brutal truth like the Sermon on the Mount.

"You have to go fill your vessel with the truth... your own story. Find your circus. You won't find it here, in the safety of these walls and this country."

My oracle, whose frail body is riddled with cancer, has me stunned in silence. When you hear the truth, your soul cannot ignore it. It rings loudly in your heart. With his wisdom and tenderness, Rodger has become my teacher not only in the arts but also in life. He is about to retire to travel the world in the little time he has left and find an ending to his own story.

As I walk out the door, he knows I won't be back.

ECHOING STARLIGHT

"Never knew my family until I chose them."

Driving from Valencia to Hollywood with the windows down and Depeche Mode blasting makes me feel alive. The Hollywood Bowl exit comes too soon, but the late-night traffic jam on the off-ramp gives me enough time to answer my phone.

"Where are you, brother?" Danny asks. "Tonight is my opening night." He talks fast and loud with a discernible Middle Eastern accent. "You're late. I have the fire marshal on my ass about to shut down the club. It's a zoo... the line is three blocks long. And Alex from WMA is here. Please, I need you. Hurry!"

"I'm almost there, brother. Don't worry, I'm getting off the exit."

Finally arriving, I think to myself that I'm always late... late. I walk up to the club, dressed like a movie star, no one would guess that my 20-year-old Honda Accord is parked two blocks away. I am one of the clued-up Hollywood hipsters and stars of the scene and probably the last subculture. I get at least a dozen compliments on my fashion sense as I make my way through the crush to the door. Anyone can pay for the clothes, if you have the money, but style is how you wear them.

The door to the club is blocked by several Samoan security guards and the fire marshal.

"No one else is getting in! Club is at capacity," one of the security guys yells on the bullhorn. "Go home!"

As security pushes back the crowd, the hulking, heavily tattooed doorman, Ricky, lifts the velvet rope and pulls me in.

"What's up, Ashe?" he shouts as the pissed-off crowd yells at him. Models you will only ever see at the producers' afterparties, and never on the covers of magazines, are posing on the red carpet. Beginner's guide to Hollywood: fake it till you make it.

"It's a madhouse out here for a Tuesday," I reply.

"Who is this fucker?!" yells some guy, 20 people deep in line. "I've got a couple of bills for you, Ricky. Let me in!"

"Didn't you hear? Go home, we're closed!" Ricky replies without even looking at the guy. He shakes my hand, smiling as he opens the door. "Saw you in a movie last weekend... whaddya working on now?"

"A film called *Fracture*, a thriller with Anthony Hopkins. But I have a night off from shooting."

"Sounds cool."

Stepping inside, the wave of heat and sound hits my face like an airplane.

"I got you, brother! Danny is waiting for you in the VIP lounge." Ricky sneakily pushes me in, unnoticed by the fire marshal.

Squeezing my way, I slowly make it through the glam traffic inside, hiding from the paparazzi. Hollywood's ripple effect is impossible to resist. The rock gods and models can suck you into their whirlpool, distorting your sense of reality. I take a while to walk over to the VIP lounge as I am stopped multiple times, needing to say "hi" to all the famous faces who recognize me. The Hollywood scene is much smaller than people realize. Here, everyone knows each other's secrets and no one's real last name.

Danny sees me in the crowd and smiles. Shaved head, dark-eyed and smiley, and a little ADD, he stops mid-sentence in a conversation with a gorgeous girl. "Ashy Ashe." He gives me a big hug. "What took you so long? Isn't this the best night ever? The bar is already at 81,000, and it's not even 11 o'clock yet," he says excitedly, moving to the beat of the music.

"Yeah, it's cool."

He ricochets from one corner of the club to another, missing nothing. When he notices a terrible song transition by the DJ, he calls over the house manager. "Get him off and put on DJ Zen! This TV amateur DJ is ruining my night."

Danny always exaggerates everything, which makes him a superb promoter. This, together with his ADD, is a gift. Before the manager can leave, Danny turns around and pushes me toward a beautiful red-headed model from NYC. "This is Michelle."

Long and leggy, she's dressed in a silky, spaghetti-strap, black dress and Christian Louboutin heels. Beneath the low lights, her flaming-red pre-Raphaelite mane shimmers against her smooth milky-white skin.

Clutching a cocktail, she flashes a gleaming smile at me. "Hey, Ashe, you're cute. How long have you known Danny?"

"I've known Ashe for 20 years," Danny cuts in. The truth is, it's more like five. We met at Coachella and have been inseparable ever since. Being nearly a decade older than me, he was the big brother I always wanted. But he's right, it feels like we've known each other for our whole lives.

"Oh my God, that's so cute." She turns and points to the four gorgeous dark-haired girls sitting at the table with Alex. "These are my girlfriends from Brazil. We're all models."

Before I have time to introduce myself to the girls, Alex stands up, arms outstretched. "Ashe, it's been a while. Good to see you."

He is dressed in a fabulously well-cut navy suit, crisp white shirt with a Louis Vuitton tie and a 18k rose-gold Rolex Daytona. He's the only person in the club wearing a suit, which is generally forbidden in the Hollywood night scene. Alex is one of the most powerful talent agents globally, currently handling celebrity bookings at William Morris Agency. I know Alex through Danny. We met during the opening night at Pure Las Vegas many years ago.

We hug and he says, "Ashe, last time I saw you, we were partying in Ibiza with Tiesto and Anton with his Russian girls at Pacha. Good times!"

"That's right. Anton... oh my God!" I smile, reminiscing about the Russian oligarch. Tall, heavyset and balding, with the cheeky baby-faced smile of a teenage boy, he was a natural charmer with the ladies because he had millions of dollars at his disposal. "Do you remember how he told the biggest drug dealer in Ibiza to come back with all the drugs he had? And the petty drug dealer came back to his beachfront mansion with two armed bodyguards, thinking Anton was gonna rob him. Do you remember the shit Anton gave him, yelling at that poor little guy? Then he threw a hundred grand at him, so he had to pick it up off the floor for offending him. Such a character. I miss him."

Alex looks at me with sad eyes. "Oh, you don't know?"

"Know what?"

"Anton is dead." Alex puts his right hand on my shoulder. "They threw him off his penthouse balcony in a hotel in Ukraine, and that's code for no cops are going to look into his murder. It's all Russian mafia shit."

"Oh man... that's terrible." My feet start feeling wobbly. I sit down in disbelief. "My heart goes out to his daughter. He was such an unbelievable character."

"Yeah, I know. There'll never be another Anton."

Before Alex can continue, Danny barges in: "This is the night I've been working for my whole life. C'mon, Ashe, you're my good luck charm. Let's have this meeting." He has his own weird superstitions.

A DJ from Lebanon, Danny came to Hollywood with dreams bigger than life. His first gig was so out-of-the-box that nobody would have ever thought it was possible. After partying all night, we'd often end up hungry at this upscale pizzeria on Beverly Boulevard. The only authentic Italian pizza place open that late. While talking to the owner, Sergio, one night, Danny said, "We'd make so much money if you allowed me to pack your joint here after hours." The owner cheerfully agreed, although he didn't believe it was possible. Up against a corner, struggling to stay open late at night, the owner often complained to us he was losing money. Sure enough, the following weekend, Danny had his DJ table set up, a doorman and valet outside. We packed the place to the rafters. Every weekend was a madhouse, trying to get into that pizza place. It became a place to be seen and an after-hours Hollywood hotspot. But Sergio's greed took over, and he started selling alcohol after 2 A.M. and lost his liquor license. Luckily for Danny, the Hollywood club owners noticed the crowds he drew and offered him promoting gigs. As his crowds and influence have grown, he's become a sort of high priest of the Hollywood club scene. His dreams of partying with celebrities have become reality, but he is always thirsting for more. He is plenty smart, inventive and, in his slacker style, ambitious, knowing exactly where he is going.

"Let's go upstairs so we can hear ourselves talk business. This is going to be life-changing." On his way to his office, we sweep past Michelle and her friends. "Girls," he tells them, "I got you a bottle of Dom. It's coming to the table. Enjoy, wait here for us. We'll be right back."

Michelle smiles, kisses him on the cheek. "Thanks, Danny, you're a star."

Danny leads us through the tight crowd upstairs to his office, where you can still feel the vibration of the bass but can hold a conversation without screaming. We all flop down on three black leather chairs, noticing the security cameras on multiple screens mounted on the wall. Danny loves to have his hand on the pulse, involved in everything he does, 110 percent.

"You ready? You ready for this bomb?" His eyes light up as he talks faster. "This is gonna be amazing. I wanna bring a big musical act to Lebanon for a huge concert."

"Lebanon?" Alex says, surprised. "Lebanon, Pennsylvania? What venue is there?"

"Noooo. Beirut, Lebanon," Danny says, like it was apparent from the start, as this is his hometown.

"Are you kidding me? You want to contract my talent to go to Beirut? And what? Get kidnapped and killed? I can't believe you're wasting my time on this! No waaaaay!" Alex raises his voice and starts gesturing with his hands. "Do you look at the news? Bush is at war in Iraq, and God knows where else in the Middle East! American contractors are getting kidnapped for ransom and sent in pieces back to their families in the US. Even after they pay the ransom. It's holy hell out there."

"Just listen," Danny persists with a smile, untouched by anything that Alex has just said. "I know America's at war with Iraq. It's destabilized the whole Middle East, and that's why the sheiks and rich people will flock to Beirut this summer."

Alex, shaking his head, looks at me in disbelief.

I don't say anything but can't help but agree with Alex. It sounds like a mad idea. Growing up in the 80s in southern Californian suburbia and constantly seeing the bombings and explosions of conflict-stricken Lebanon beamed across the news cycle, I see it as this surreal, ceaseless war zone, synonymous with terrorists and kidnappings. After the suicide bombings of a US marine barracks in 1983, American citizens were forbidden from traveling to the country for a decade until the travel ban was lifted in 1997.

"It's the Paris of the Middle East. And this summer, it's the Soccer World Cup." Danny gets even more excited, confident he can close this deal. "Thousands are going to party, and this concert will be the epicenter that everyone will talk about. We'll be kings."

Alex's body starts to relax and he leans in, listening intently now.

"I worked my whole life for this moment. This is the biggest opportunity for us to go bigger than THIS," Danny says, gesturing at the club. "Look at my friend Paul. He started Coachella when everybody said people in LA wouldn't drive to middle of the desert to some Indio city for a festival. Look at Pasquale, he started

Electric Daisy Carnival in Vegas. This is the future. We need to get out of the clubs and go bigger!"

"Sounds good, but these concerts are in the safety of the United States of fucking America—"

"You want safety?" Danny cuts him off. "My dad is a retired general of the Lebanese army. Tell your artist we're gonna have the Lebanese army with tanks guarding the venue."

Alex, whose close-cropped peppery hair and heavily tanned skin make him look older than his 30-odd years, leans more forward on the couch, intrigued but still unconvinced. "Which American artist is gonna risk their life to perform in the Middle East right now?"

Danny, with his earnest intensity, grins as 50 Cent's "In Da Club" comes on, and we see the crowd going wild on the security cameras. The entire club seems to be moving to the beat of the song. He opens the door to allow the music to drift in.

"If the money's right, a gangster who's been shot at multiple times," Danny says, finally piquing Alex's interest. Pointing to the camera screens, he sings along with the lyrics: "If they hate, then let 'em hate and watch the money pile up."

I'm amazed watching the mood in the room take a turn. This is classic Danny at his best.

Alex laughs and claps his hands together. "You know what, Danny, 50 Cent is the biggest act right now. He sold eight million copies of this record and he's one tough hustler."

"That's why he's perfect. If I'm gonna do it, I'm doing it big."

"Fuck you, Danny," he says with a laugh. "This might cost

me my career. This is gonna cost a lot. I need a private jet to and from, three penthouse suites at your best hotel, a particular rider, and 50 Cent's rate is 350 grand for three hours. You wanna risk half a million on your outrageous idea?"

Danny shoots me a glance. "Ashe, do you believe in me? You think I should do it?"

I look at him as I hear the 50 Cent tune shaking his office, thinking the way this whole situation is unfolding is some divine intervention. "Life's too short to live with regrets. You should do it."

Danny extends his hand out to Alex to close the deal.

Staring at him drop-jawed, Alex flops back against the sofa, grunting and holding his head. Laughs as he finally gathers himself to shake Danny's hand. "Only you, you crazy motherfucker, can put me in this position and still have me smiling. It better be big, with no casualties! I'll have contracts written for you."

"I'll call my investors tonight. We're going to Beirut, baby!" Danny shouts, outstretching his arms toward me.

"Whoa, we?! No. You're going to Beirut," I reply, now realizing he brought me here to close two deals.

"I'm not doing this without you, brother. You're my lucky rabbit's foot, and this is the biggest gamble. I'm not going without you."

"I'm an American, I don't want to die in the Middle East."

"You've never been to Middle East. What they've shown you on the news is all propaganda... bullshit!"

"Not sure about that."

"Beirut is not this scary, dark place full of terrorists. That's not my hometown. You must see it to believe it. You think Vegas is the ultimate nightlife? Wait till you party in Beirut."

The look in his eyes can only make me smile, and I suddenly remember Rodger Henderson's words, *"Go find your story."*

MOTHER'S COMET POWDER

"It's our safety nets that keep us trapped."

Dolce & Gabbana white collared shirt, Hermès leather belt, Versace boxers, Chrome Hearts leather wristband, True Religion jeans with a Buddha embroidered on the back pocket. These are the first of many items that I'm taking out of my squeaky closets. Perfectly folded and laid out on my bed. I am carefully packing my designer threads into a large Louis Vuitton bag. My OCD is in full effect. I must've inherited it from my biological father, who's one of the best urologists in Colombia. At least that's what my mother has told me, although I wouldn't know, as I've only seen him a handful of times in my life.

"Why are you making all this noise?" My mother opens my bedroom door and peeks in. She doesn't allow me to have a lock on my door because she reminds me every day that this is her house and I'm just a guest.

I had a very nomadic lifestyle, flitting between LA, New York and Europe. I moved back with my parents into the house where I grew up in Valencia, a peaceful, palm-fringed suburb outside of LA. We live in a ranch-style house with a backyard filled with lemon trees, bird of paradise and jasmine and honeysuckle vines whose sweet, heady fragrance drifts into my bedroom in the evenings. Only a half-an-hour's drive from LA, it is a perfect base, and my mom and stepdad are happy to see me more often. Since leaving CalArts six years ago, I got a Hollywood agent who gets me pretty near-constant acting gigs.

Scanning the room with her hawk eyes, she says, "What are all these clothes? What are you packing for?"

"Have you seen my passport, Mom?" I reply, too busy to notice that she's inspecting my room with her nosiness.

"Where are you going that you need your passport?"

"On a trip." Rule number one of dealing with my mother is to be as vague as possible and not volunteer any specific information. It will only come back to bite you in the ass later. But she continues to pull on the rope.

"What trip? This is the first time I'm hearing about a trip?" She realizes by the size of my luggage that this isn't for work or one of my frequent weekends to Vegas or Miami.

"With Danny." I'm trying hard, and against my OCD, this is the time to pack faster before she assaults me with more questions. If there's anyone who can sabotage my trip, it's my mother.

"You're not getting your passport until you tell me where you're going!"

Oh, fuck. I've clearly lost round one, and I'm about to lose the second. I pretend not to hear the question, rushing to the bathroom to get my toothbrush and toiletries. She follows me like a shadow.

"Steve! I am your mother. You answer me when I'm talking to you," she shouts as I pass her in the hallway back to my room. She always calls me by my birth name when she's mad. She's never forgiven me that I legally changed it, disavowing my heritage. Carrying the last name of someone who did not raise me as I got older seemed futile. Out of that pain, I rose like a phoenix. Changing my first name to Ashe is the reminder of the pain I burned and left behind.

"What's all the commotion?" In walks my stepdad, a man of few words, highly educated and easygoing. My pop didn't have to, but he raised another man's son as his own. I had an endearing respect for him for loving me, even though he always took my mom's side.

"He's packing on some trip and won't let me know where he's going?"

"Mom, I'm 28 years old... not a kid."

"If you're living in our house, you're obligated to inform us where you're going because we're responsible for you," says Pop calmly with conviction. "We raised you better than that."

Shit! I lost round two. Here we go into round three. They ganged up on me. Still, despite my conventional upbringing, they are pretty cool parents. When I went through the typical suburban kid rebellion of growing my hair long, inking my arms and sneaking out at night to hit the clubs when the grunge thing was peaking, they took it in stride. But I have a good feeling this is about to get ugly. *Where did I put my passport?* I need to finish packing, take a quick shower and get out to the airport—or else I'll never leave.

"I'm helping Danny with a concert." I'd rather avoid a direct answer than tell a lie.

"Where are you going?" my mother shouts as I continue to hold my ground, staying silent.

"Answer your mother!" my pop insists.

"Lebanon. Danny's already there. He's waiting for me!" I say firmly as I stake my flag on the moon. I'm done packing and just need to take a shower. Hoping my stern tone will bring their questions to a pause.

"LEBANON?!" My mom is visibly distraught. "What are you thinking, my son?"

"It'll be okay."

"It's not okay! It's dangerous!"

My pop, usually agreeing with her anyway, thinks it's an outlandish idea.

I know she's right. While Beirut may be cosmopolitan and by far the most liberal of Arab cities, it is in the midst of an insanely repressive and turbulent region. Only the year before, in 2005, the former Lebanese Prime Minister Rafiq Hariri was assassinated in a car bombing, alongside other multiple terrorist attacks.

She goes on, "I have enough to worry about with my health and don't need to be living in fear that my son might be kidnapped or beheaded."

My desire for adventure eclipses the risks. I could easily get shot and killed in LA or anywhere else. But little do I know how prescient her words are.

Hopefully she stops here and doesn't blame me for another sickle-cell crisis. My mother, who is half-Chinese and half-black Colombian, has sickle-cell anemia.

"My chest is hurting. You're going to be the death of me! My sickle cell cannot take so much stress. Why are you doing this to me?" She's now shouting as I realize I've lost round three. Here we go. I need to astral project my mind out of here because the shit has hit the fan and is about to land in my ears.

"I just had a blood transfusion last week, and you're going to make me go into crisis again. You have no mercy for your mother!" She continues her assaults. My mom is a classic narcissist. Everything is about her, *always*. If I'm going to a war-torn region and potentially threatening my life, it's about how it makes her feel. I love her, but sometimes I don't think she can show love back.

Before I leap into the shower, I suddenly remember where I left my passport. I run back to my room, open my desk's hidden drawer and hide my passport quickly in my luggage.

Just as I am walking back to the bathroom, my mom, like a snow blower, is shaking an entire can of Comet powder onto the shower floor, yelling, "You're not leaving this house until this bathroom is spotless!"

Round four is lost. My mom's way of showing love is definitely unconventional. In a normal mother-and-son goodbye, this would be the time for a long embrace, but Comet powder is the equivalent in my mother's mind. She sits on the toilet, watching me clean every spot. She never cries. After cleaning the bathroom, I don't have time to shower. I grab my luggage.

On my way out the door, Lebanon bound, I dust off the Comet powder from my clothes.

CEDAR TREES OF PARIS

"Eyes shut...Following the dots..."

I wake up to the pilot's announcement just as we're about to land in Beirut. Through the fluffy white clouds, I can see the city's jagged coastline and the bluey-green glimmer of the Mediterranean Sea. The view is beautiful and unexpected. It almost looks like California from this high up. I have now traveled farther than anyone in my family has ever been away from home. The excitement of why I'm here and seeing my best friend in a few moments outweighs the feeling of any fear I had stepping onto this Lufthansa flight or any pain the odd goodbye with my parents have caused. As we're descending over Beirut, I notice a beautiful red roof in a sharp shape of a cross next to a massive building with turquoise domes and four thin, tall towers surrounding it. The red cross is a church built with a similar floor plan to those churches you see in Paris. I wonder what the other building could be.

Once we land, there's a strange feeling of familiarity as I notice this airport is as busy as LAX. Almost feeling at home until the customs army officer asks me what I'm doing in Lebanon and how long I plan to stay. I'm taken aback by his directness. I tell him I'm part of the group organizing the 50 Cent concert.

"Ah, you're the ones that are bringing 50 Cent," he says, smiling. "Welcome, Mr. Ashe, to Lebanon. I wish you prosperity in your venture." He stamps my passport and motions for the next visitor to come up to the window.

Walking toward the baggage claim, I'm relieved he didn't press me for the return date since I don't have one. Just like Danny, I came here on a one-way ticket.

I wander out into the blazing-white sunshine amid the clusters of cars, repetitious horn sounds and the loud chatter of the city. There's no one policing this traffic. I see a biker zigzagging between the vehicles in the opposite direction, a harried mother with a toddler and big luggage crossing the street, shouting for cars to move so she can squeeze between them. Taxis parked bumper to bumper, literally on the sidewalk. One driver is screaming at another over a passenger like a pair of hyenas scrapping over a kill. This chaos is a reminder I'm no longer in the States. I miss the LAPD and some sort of order at this very moment.

I feel hundreds of gazes on me while standing on the street. Here, the way I'm dressed sticks out like a sore thumb. Suddenly, I feel someone grab my left hand, which is holding on to my Louis

Vuitton bag. It's a taxi driver pulling me toward his car parked on the sidewalk.

"*Habibi, habibi,* come, come! I take you!" he says in thickly accented broken English, dragging me to his taxi as he pops the trunk with his other hand.

"I'm here for Danny. I'm waiting for my friend." I pull my hand and bag away from his sweaty grip.

"Yes, Danny, Danny, Danny, Yes! I take you!" he reassures me as he tries to snatch my bag away again and put it into his trunk.

"You know Danny? Did he send you?" I say, confused. "He said he was going to pick me up himself."

"Danny, Danny, yes, yes. I take you, Dannieee," he says, smiling and nodding his head repeatedly. Before he gets the chance to grab on to my bag again, I hear my name from a distance. It's Danny, holding up a giant white board with *Welcome Justin Timberlake* written on it. Danny's sarcastic sense of humor puts a smile on my face amid this chaos.

He runs over through the crowd, screaming, "Ashe, whaddya doing, *habibi*? Are you trying to get lost?" He turns toward the taxi driver and yells at him in Arabic. As he ushers me away to his parked car, they have a chuckle. Danny appreciates a good hustle. I feel relieved in the safety of my best friend's presence.

"What does *habibi* mean?" I ask as we near his green BMW 850 CSI.

"It means you... my best friend. It's a term of endearment."

"It has a nice ring to it. I like it, *habibi*."

As we laugh, a 20-something-year-old man with a ponytail and Ray-Ban shades comes out of the driver's side. He's wearing white linen trousers and an eye-popping pastel shirt, something you might see on the old *Miami Vice* show. He opens the trunk and puts my luggage inside.

"Hi, I'm Teddy." He hugs me firmly. It appears to be a regular custom to invade people's personal space here.

"Ashe, this is my assistant, Teddy. Teddy, this is my best friend in the entire world. I have good news for you, Ashe will attract the most beautiful women in Lebanon."

Teddy breaks into a wide smile.

"The ladies fall crazy in love with this one," Danny exaggerates, as usual. "Look at 'im, six-foot-one, with those high cheekbones, bronze skin and almond eyes, he's a real heartbreaker."

Glancing at Teddy, I flush with embarrassment and roll my eyes.

"I can't believe my best friend is here, where I grew up. Mr. Hollywood in Beirut. This is once in a lifetime. Let's do this, *habibi*."

Pulling out of the airport, before getting onto the highway, we whiz past a huge, impossible-to-miss 50 Cent concert billboard with Danny's name blazing at the top corner.

Danny elbows me. "Look, Ashe, I told you we're going to be kings out here... it's just the beginning."

Teddy turns up the radio, driving faster toward the center of the city. We hear the DJ on the radio announcing a 50 Cent concert by Danny B coming to Beirut on June 10th. As the car zooms through labyrinthine streets with a mix of Arabesque, Venetian Gothic centuries-old mosques, churches and palazzos and glossy glass-and-steel skyscrapers and brutalist mid-century towers, almost every billboard I see is an ad for Danny B's 50 Cent concert at the Beirut International Exhibition & Leisure Center, commonly known as BIEL. I feel like I'm in the twilight zone, overwhelmed by the gravity of the possibility of the upcoming success. Advertising like that in the US would cost tens of millions of dollars. I've seen nothing like this. It's understandable now, from a cost perspective, why he wanted to do it in Beirut so badly.

The streets are filled with bustle and noise. It's early spring and the trees are in full bloom, flowers and vines tumbling from cobbled courtyards and balconies. The purple and red jacaranda flame against the sky and oleander and orange blossoms perfume the air. Many of the old buildings, grand and gorgeously ornate, are still scarred and pockmarked from the civil war, which ended in the 90s. I look to my left and see the red cross roof church and the turreted, turquoise-domed sandstone structure next to it, which I think is the exact one I saw from the plane.

"What's that building?" I ask Danny.

"That is the Blue Mosque. The most beautiful mosque in Lebanon. And the church next to it is the Maronite Cathedral of St. George. Only in Lebanon can you see a Christian church and a Muslim mosque next door to each other like this, *habibi*," he explains. "It's a symbol of hope that maybe one day peace, and not war, will be humankind's choice."

The size and the beauty of both places of worship are breathtaking. Hardly what I've recently heard of the war in Iraq, which is a stark contrast to what I am seeing. With that and all the prejudices against Muslims I've seen in the movies and learned growing up as a Catholic in America, I never thought peace between two religions would exist. What a beautiful sight.

"Are we staying in this area?" I ask Danny as we cruise through the quiet, leafy streets with blossoming trees, dilapidated villas and stylish boutiques and cafés.

"No, *habibi*, we're not staying downtown but driving to the Christian side... to Jounieh. It's a beautiful coastal city, where I grew up."

"What do you mean, Christian side?"

"It's in Lebanon as it was for thousands of years. Religion separates our communities. The Sunni Muslims live in north Lebanon, the Shia Muslims in the south, and a sprinkle of Christians in the middle. Strangely, that's how we've learned to coexist peacefully."

"Wow. How did it feel growing up being a religious minority?"

"Oh, *habibi*, we are *not* a minority," he corrects me in his Danny B confident way. "Over 50 percent of Lebanese are Christian. But if you ask me how it felt, it felt great. Christians are the rock stars of this country. We party, we drink, we eat what we want and pray when we want. I consider us the bad boys that everyone wants to be."

"You just can't marry outside of your religion," Teddy cuts in. "That's strictly forbidden. You could get killed for that and no one would bat an eyelash."

"Damn, that's harsh," I say, realizing again how far I am from home.

Cruising down the coast to Danny's hometown, I find a similarity between the Lebanese Highway 51 and California's Pacific Coast Highway 1. The beach to my left is so close that I can see the sparkling blue waters of the Mediterranean. For one of the oldest settled lands in our human history, the waters are still stunningly clear. In an instant, it makes me sad thinking of the contrast between Lebanon and California and how we've polluted this planet beyond recognition in America. The oil spills, the contaminated sands, the floating plastic, the putrid smell are what I've witnessed as our contribution to the earth. Yet humans have occupied these beaches here for thousands of years, and they still hold magic, looking untouched by benighted men.

We pull off Highway 51 into Jounieh, a bustling beach town that immediately looks like a rich man's toy box filled with shiny yachts and sailboats. Just north of Beirut, this former sleepy fishing village that was once surrounded by banana plantations and citrus groves has been transformed into a party place, teeming with chic boutique hotels, restaurants and nightclubs. The little side-street cafés, draped in jasmine and full of charm, remind me of Paris in the spring and summer. The hustle and bustle intertwined with the laughter of people enjoying a glass of wine while socializing with strangers resembles the western world. On the other side, the lush-green cedar-cloaked hills look as if they are pushing down on the human dwellings to disallow our invasion of the mountain. A view you'd never see in America, where mountains are removed so the rich can have a better view from their mansions. Passing a row of beautiful stone apartment blocks and storefronts hugging the shore, we park off the Rue Principale in a dirt parking lot behind a whitewashed six-story building, its ornate balconies with vivid splashes of bougainvillea spilling over the iron railings. I step up onto one of the hundreds of giant stone boulders. Looking down, I face the shimmering aquamarine of the sea. The water is so clear that I can see the seashells and jewel-bright fish in the shallows. I take out my SONY Cyber-shot and snap a few photos just as the sun sets. Even the pinkish-orange sunset kind of reminds me of home, the way it falls into water as it does in Malibu.

"*Habibi!*" Danny B screams at me from the white building's entrance as Teddy passes him, carrying my luggage inside. "Come back to reality! Enough daydreaming. Let's go, I have a surprise for you."

The broken elevator forces us to climb the spiral stone staircase up to the sixth floor. The climb drags on like a nosebleed, but the staggering view through the open oak door of the condo is worth it. My jaw hits the floor as I step inside the three-bedroom, two-balcony penthouse. The breezy white high-ceilinged space with polished tiled floors has tons of natural light and two balconies set between two seas: on the west, the Mediterranean; and on the east, the sea of cedar trees.

"Dude, I thought you said this was a chalet?" I say to Danny, laughing. "This is a big-ass legit penthouse."

"Well, I call it a chalet... I like the sound of that word." He shrugs and shows me my room.

"This is sweet," I say, glimpsing the glorious view of green cedars against a vivid blue sky, the crashing waves below. I go straight to the windows and swing them open to the balmy sea air, soaking it all in.

"Shut the blinds and get some rest. In a couple hours, my beautiful surprise for you will arrive."

"What did you do?"

"Aww, Ashe, you're my best mate. You'll thank me later." He leaves the room, closing the door behind him.

My senses are in overload, and the jet lag just hits me. I take a quick shower, as my OCD would never allow me to lie in bed with travel grime all over me. I lie down on the bed, hypnotized by the swaying of the cedars and the singsong of the cicadas, and drift away.

HEART OF STEEL

"When all the money in the world is not enough... "

An enormous wave slams against the boulders under my balcony and wakes me. It's dusk outside and the tide is in. It feels very late, like that feeling you might have slept through a couple of days. I rush to my feet, dizzy, and open the door. Down the hallway, I hear Danny's voice speaking in Arabic with someone. Walking into the room, I see he's speaking to a man in a white thobe and sandals. He looks somewhere in his 20s, fit, dark, clean-cut, Middle Eastern.

"There he is, the sleeping beauty," Danny says in mid-conversation. "All you need to be fully awake is your princess's kiss. She's on her way and will be here in ten minutes."

Dazed and confused, I stand there, thinking I am still dreaming. "Who? What princess?"

"Hi, I'm Abdul," says the meticulously groomed man in the white thobe. "I heard a lot about you."

Danny introduces us before I have the time to answer. "Abdul is my new business partner for some side projects I want to do before the concert. He's from Qatar and very rich, oil money. Abdul will be staying here with us."

Danny's new friend seems to enjoy this introduction as he sits on the couch, grinning, with his legs crossed. He takes a sip of his tea, and his clunky gold watch on his skinny wrist is impossible not to notice.

"It's a pleasure meeting you." I lean forward to give him a hug, since this seems to be a normal custom here.

"*As-Salaam-Alaikum*," Abdul replies, reciprocating the hug and smelling of strong cologne.

"I was just about to wake you up," Danny says, smiling, without answering any of my questions. "You better get ready. She doesn't like to wait."

"Okay, but you have to give me the info," I murmur, still jet-lagged, knowing he's already set me up with someone extraordinary.

"You go get ready and I'll fill you in." He follows me into my room.

"So, what am I doing?" I open my suitcase, unclear what I should I be wearing.

"*Habibi*, you're about to go on a date with one of the richest girls in all the Middle East," Danny says with pride in his voice.

"What's the big deal? We both know I dated some of the richest girls in Hollywood."

"Lemme stop you right there. I've seen you date famous models, actresses and, yes, women with millions, but you've never dated a billionaire."

I'm speechless.

"Yes, *habibi*, you're going on a date with a billionaire. You better not fuck this up because we'd love for her to invest in our projects as well. If you get this right, we'll have a beautiful summer."

"Oh, man. Come on."

"It's a level of living that you cannot comprehend. Please don't break her heart."

"Is this why you invited me here? I don't wanna go on a blind date with some spoiled Lebanese princess." I abandon my search for clothes and slump on the bed, refusing to be pimped in Beirut.

Abdul rushes into the room to let us know there's a Mercedes McLaren downstairs, frantically beeping. Danny smirks and says, "Just put on your shoes. It's game time."

"Danny, I don't have the money to take out a billionaire for a dinner. I don't wanna go."

"Here, take my Amex. If you need to, use it! But, *habibi*, trust me. You won't need to."

"Now hurry, get up, because she doesn't like to wait for anyone," Danny says as he unbuttons a few buttons on my shirt.

I give him a dirty look. "Oh, for fuck's sake, you're like my mother."

"What good are chest muscles if you don't show 'em. Show the goods, man. Go, go, go." He pushes me out the door.

While walking down six flights of these spiraling cement stairs, a lot goes through my head. I've dated rich and strong-minded women before. It seems to be the type that I'm attracted to, but they can also be a very toxic kind of relationship. I remember Anna, my first real relationship. I was 16 and she was a decade older. She was the boyhood crush that I never thought would be possible. In my experience, rich women lead you down bottomless rabbit holes, whether you can survive making it out. After four years of having my heart chopped up into a million pieces, it felt great to be free of her and the toxicity she brought into my life. That was my first lesson of love. After that, I had the skin of a crocodile and the heart of a bird. The last steps are the hardest. My curiosity propels me forward while my heart wants to fly back upstairs. The honk is so loud I can only imagine what kind of bitchy, demanding woman is pushing on that horn so ferociously.

I stride up to the matte-black Mercedes McLaren with black-tinted windows. Damn, I can't see inside but can feel her eyes sizing me up. I feel like I'm being examined in an interrogation room. I've heard that a woman knows if she wants to sleep with you within the first ten seconds of meeting you. Damn, it's taking me over ten seconds to figure out how to open this door. I seriously look like an idiot, fumbling around the edges of this car, and to my surprise the door flips up and not to the side, so I nearly end up with a chin laceration when it finally opens. I smile, trying to hide my embarrassment, but my cheeks are already red.

"Hi," I say as she smiles.

"Hi, Ashe. I'm Amira," she says in a raspy voice, with a thick Middle Eastern accent.

I'm trying to sit, but there's a huge red Birkin bag in the passenger seat. She gestures me in but doesn't move her bag. I get the hint: the bag is going on my lap. *What the fuck.* I already feel like a second-class citizen.

"I heard you just got in. Did you have a pleasant flight?"

I close the door as she speeds away toward the city to the beat of her classic 80s music.

"Actually, I did. I slept most of the way," I reply, watching her shift through the gears as frantically as she was honking the horn minutes earlier.

"I've actually met you before. Do you remember me?" Amira asks, switching into fifth gear. I hope this is the last gear this car has, as we're already past 100 MPH. The whiplash makes me feel like a crash-test dummy.

We're careening down the narrow roads in her supercar risking life and limb, with motorbikes weaving in and out of the dusty traffic in front of us. The streets, wild and chaotic, are a free-for-all, with cars and motorbikes racing through red lights and tearing past as though they were on a racetrack.

"Sorry, I don't recall, but the Hollywood scene is small." I clutch the Birkin bag, scared for my life. She is definitely trying to show off.

"No, no, no. My sister and I flew our jet to Las Vegas last year to join you guys for New Year's Eve at Pure Nightclub," she says in a voice laced with contempt as she pushes harder on the gas pedal.

"Aren't you afraid of getting pulled over for speeding?"

"Honey, this is Beirut. There are no sheriffs here." She laughs. I get pushed farther into the seat from the sudden acceleration. I realize my fear is fueling her aggressive driving. It's turning her on because she's in power. Control is something she doesn't want me to have.

"Your Birkin and I may not make it tonight," I joke, trying to turn the tables on her. She laughs with her raspy voice, almost like a man. "I don't know how I would've forgotten your face, or your voice."

"Well, I don't know about my face, but, honey, I've heard many times that my voice can scare certain men."

"Actually, your driving scares me way more than your voice."

"In the steel industry, I have to deal with powerful men who run countries. Girls with sweet voices get eaten alive by those sharks," she replies, her voice getting even deeper.

"I suppose that's a wonderful asset to have for someone who has to negotiate under those conditions."

"No one has ever said that to me. That takes some insight. I like you. But I'm not happy that you don't remember me. Although you seemed pretty preoccupied with THAT girl at the time."

I may not remember Amira, but I remember that past New Year's Eve. I was dating Jenn, which is probably why I wasn't paying attention to any other woman. Jenn had a way of captivating anyone in her company, which made her a perfect candidate for her job. She was the premier VIP host at Caesars Palace Pure Nightclub. She was over six feet tall, with sparkling blue eyes, jet-black hair and an innocent face with a straw heart, straight from Iowa. Pure was the first grand nightclub in any casino, and VIP hosts and promoters made ridiculous bank. She would speed me around town in her red Ferrari F430, had a luxurious penthouse apartment off the strip and, oddly enough, kept all of her cash in a giant hefty bag hidden in her stove. Hundreds of thousands of dollars that she couldn't put into a bank account to avoid the IRS. The nightlife pays well, but it's short-lived, just like our relationship.

Now that I'm traveling at over 130 MPH, my past seems like a hallucination against the backdrop of the Mediterranean waves. Amira's voice is so distant at this moment that I can't understand what she's saying. And she realizes it and brakes suddenly, which snaps me out of my daydream, sending her Birkin bag flying onto the dashboard.

She grabs the bag and puts it back on my lap and says, "We're here."

As we make the roundabout in downtown Beirut, I see the restaurant ahead on the right-hand side. It's kind of hard to miss, with the amount of luxury cars wrapped around the entire block. Amira pulls into the orange Spanish-style restaurant as close to the entrance as humanly possible, narrowly missing the valet guys. She revs the engine one more time in a grand announcement that she has arrived, snatches the Birkin off my lap and waits for the valet to open our doors. The row of dinner guests, high on the balcony seating overlooking the sea, turn their heads and watch our every move as we ascend the stone stairs to the maître d'.

I quickly pat down my pants to ensure that Danny's credit card is still in my pocket. The gorgeous hostess kindly asks for the name on the reservation. Amira ignores her and sweeps past as a man in a tuxedo greets her with a kiss on the cheek. He must be the owner, I think to myself. They talk for a short while in Arabic, her eyes sweeping around the swanky, warmly lit restaurant.

She compliments him in English on the decor and ambiance as he leads us to our table in the middle of the restaurant, which is not surprising, watching her revel in the attention she receives. I can feel a thousand eyes on me. Amira is unhappy because our table has four chairs and she wants a more intimate set-up and only by the fountain. The owner babbles something in Arabic and four employees set up the table right where she wants it. She insists they move the table a few feet away from the fountain because she doesn't want to get wet.

The owner pulls out the seat for her and mentions he has a delicious bottle of Dom on the wine list. Amira says that's fine and requests our special dinner, which is off the menu, without asking me what I want to eat.

For the first time, I scrutinize her features. She is in her mid-20s, shoulder-length bob, exquisite makeup, and dressed as if she had a team of stylists put her together for a fashion shoot. Her short, swirly flower-print cocktail dress showcases her voluptuous body. She's like a Lebanese Monica Bellucci.

"This is a gorgeous restaurant, and you look flawless tonight," I say, happy that Danny has set me up with her.

"Of course, honey," she says with a twinkle in her dark-brown eyes, leaning forward and exposing more of her beautiful breasts. "You don't know. Everyone's looking at us."

"Really, why?"

"If you think the Hollywood scene is small. Honey, the Beirut scene is much smaller," she says, raising a well-sculpted black eyebrow. "All these people, they all know who I am, but not who you are. They're all probably whispering to each other, 'Where the hell did she get him from?'"

LOVE HAS NO RELIGION

"To start a fire, you will always need air..."

The mellow candlelit evening is going very well. The first three of six courses were delicious and contained the same key ingredient: bread. It doesn't take us long to move on to the second bottle of Dom. It's been a while since I've seen a woman so meticulously put together. Amira's peep-toe designer heels flaunt her flawless pedicure while her French-manicured hands spread her exotic perfume in the air as she gestures. She holds her champagne glass with a sense of aristocracy, with her diamond Cartier bracelet and rose-gold Rolex dangling around her tiny wrist. She definitely knows her place in this society.

I need to give credit when it is due. Danny came through with Amira. It has not always been this way. Often when a friend sets up these types of blind dates, it ends up in disaster. The

Lebanese sea breeze feels warm against my skin and whisks me back to the evening Coachella desert air when I first met Danny.

In 2001, walking up to the festival entrance gate, I was part of a small group. That April, I was 23, slowly building an acting career and bristling with youthful energy. My girlfriend Cheryl, a spirited neo-flowerchild-chick, looking very 1967 in a crochet minidress and daisy crown, brought her three closest friends and lots of psychedelic mushrooms. I'd done ecstasy before but never mushrooms. They kept hyping it up on the two-hour drive from LA to INDIO, CA.

At the front of the line, a group of police officers patted everyone down as the crowd entered the polo fields for the one-day festival. Realizing this, Cheryl instructed all of us to just finish all the mushrooms before they got confiscated. By the time we reached the front of the line, we were all so high we had to go sit in a circle in the front lawn area. Between the mushrooms and triple-digit desert heat, I have no recollection of how many hours we must have sat there before Cheryl came up with the bright idea of going inside to actually enjoy the concert.

With the sun dipping behind the high desert mountains, we wandered through the palm tree gates into a wonderland of music and art in a copious grass field. Jane's Addiction was head-lining and at that moment the Dandy Warhols, a cool Portland indie-rock band, were playing, but we hardly noticed in our druggy haze. Coachella was much smaller in 2001, a proper indie festival giving way to an open polo field, unobstructed by crowds. This allowed my free spirit to run, dance, rage and burn like a

Roman candle. In my psychedelic trance, I separated myself from the group. Covered in sweat and tears of joy, my long-haired wig seemed to become a part of me, sticking to my bare chest and back. Shirtless, the only piece of clothing that mattered to me was the green military pants I got from a designer in LA who went to Vietnam and reused the abandoned fatigues of the American soldiers for his clothing line. I felt I was dancing for someone who no longer could. When the music stopped, I wandered pointlessly.

"There, there he is!" I heard a woman's voice shouting. I turned around and standing on the white lawn chair in the VIP area beside a hipster couple was Cheryl, waving for me to rejoin her. As I got closer, I gave her a sweet hug.

"Who's that guy?" I heard a man say with an accent. I turned around toward the cheerful, energetic voice. And there he was, D Bizzle, grinning and seeming to enjoy the moment sitting with a gorgeous Spanish model in all white on his lap.

"This is my boyfriend, Danny." Cheryl introduced me. "The one I've been telling you about."

"So glad to meet you. Look at you," Danny said, looking me up and down. "Love your tattoos. We saw you dancing out in the field. I was like Whoa!" He gestured to the group of 30-something people surrounding him. "This handsome motherfucker is crazy, boys. Hold on to your girls," he said with his soft Middle Eastern accent, then laughed. To be complimented like this by another man, you know you're dealing with someone very confident.

"You saw me dancing in the darkness of this field, but I was praying. Praying for more moments like these in my life. And you are a part of an answer to that prayer, so I appreciate you. I see you, Danny," I replied, still flying on mushrooms, in an entirely different state of mind than he was.

"*What?!* That is some deep shit! I like your boyfriend a lot, Cheryl," Danny said, surprised and half-laughing as he stood up. "You guys have to come to my after-party tonight. Follow us. We're staying at the Ritz-Carlton. We booked the entire hotel. I'll have a room for you guys if you wanna stay the night."

"Really, Danny? We'd love to! Yay!" Cheryl replied excitedly and guided me to follow behind Danny's group.

As the sun in the Rancho Mirage desert illuminated the sky the following morning, it also shined a ray of light into my life: Danny. We have been inseparable ever since.

"So, do you like it?" Amira says, annoyed, snapping me out of another daydream.

"Excuse me?" I reply dozily. "Do I like what?"

"Do you enjoy living in America?" she repeats with a hint of annoyance in her voice. A girl who definitely can't stand being ignored.

"It's my home, obviously."

Amira leans in and switches her crossed leg to the other side. She arches her back, places her elbows on the table like a lioness looking at the prey across the Serengeti. "Did you come to make Lebanon your home? It would be a significant improvement."

I just laugh. "You've been to Las Vegas. Do you honestly believe Beirut is a notable improvement?"

"Yes, I've been to Las Vegas, and I couldn't wait to come home."

"I see you as a Middle Eastern woman in a white America, and no matter your wealth, I see how you would be glad to run back to Lebanon, especially during these times of war and chaos. There's so much division between our two cultures. We may never see eye to eye, but there's only one home for everyone. And as many beautiful countries as I visit and enjoy, nothing will take away this one truth for me. America is where I was born and it'll always be my home. Is Lebanon some utopian promise land?"

"Trust me, honey, you'll see how caged your precious so-called 'freedom' is," she replies, her voice rising and getting deeper. "I'm going to teach you what it means to live, American. And then you tell me where you want your home to be."

"That sounds like a gift, a curse, or both." I say, curious to find out what she means.

The server comes to ask if we need anything else. She asks for the bill, and he tells her the owner has taken care of it. Funny, a free $2,000 meal for a billionaire? The irony doesn't escape me. As she is getting up from the table, I thank the server with a $300 tip.

She sees it and says, "Honey, that is unnecessary."

"It may not be necessary, but it could be needed," I reply, smiling at her as I shake the server's hand.

"I like you. Okay, let's go. *Yallah*!" she says, laughing. "To the next stop, the night is still young."

Drifting from place to place and partying like it's the last night on earth seems to be the thing to do in Beirut. With our destination unclear to me, we race away toward the metropolitan part of the city. She seems to be enjoying herself and keeps smiling at me and throttling faster in her black batmobile. I can hear the loud music a block away as we approach her next mystery stop. She swerves virtually onto the pavement alongside a large beige stone building, packed with people waiting outside next to some of the most expensive cars I've ever seen in one place. Again, she sweeps through the crowd like everyone knows her. I follow behind in awe, watching these big men and beautiful women make way for her to pass, like Moses parting the Red Sea. The doorman notices her, smiles, and greets her while she clasps my hand for the first time and pulls me close behind her. Her hands are soft and warm, but with a firm grip. She turns around and smiles, seeing my reaction as we walk through the golden double doors into the nightclub.

"Do you miss your Vegas now?" She laughs, not caring if I respond, so I don't. I just smile back.

The nightclub is jammed with stunningly beautiful people, clad in Cavalli, Armani and Versace, drinking, smoking and dancing their hearts out on the tables. They're all dressed like it's Paris Fashion Week, while I'm the only one in jeans, a white collared shirt and sneakers. I feel everyone sizing me up again.

Moving through the crowd up the stairs to the balconied area to Amira's table, I see a familiar face.

Thrilled to see me, Danny screams over the loud music, "*Habibi!* You made it." We embrace with great excitement at the huge VIP table with a small crowd of Amira's glam rich friends, who speak a mishmash of English, Arabic and French, all awaiting her arrival.

"Did I ever tell you, you're my best friend in the universe," I say to Danny with a huge smile. "You hooked me up good this time. Amira is a character."

"She's a lioness. You gotta be careful. Men fear her. I repeat, do not break her heart."

"DB, it was like playing chess all evening at dinner. You have no idea."

"Lemme tell you how my evening went," Danny replies and pulls me to the side for a more private conversation. I can feel Amira's eyes on us as we move to the corner of her extensive VIP section. "I had to drive to the south of Beirut into straight-up forbidden Shite territory."

"Why would you ever go down there?"

"I was picking up the most beautiful girl in all of Lebanon."

"You risked your life for a girl?"

"It's not just any girl. She's a Miss Lebanon runner-up, and I'm in love with her." Danny drops unexpected news on me.

"I'm floored. In all my years as your best friend, this is the first time I'm hearing you're in love with someone. She must be spectacular in and out and in bed," I reply, scanning the table for anyone fitting her description.

"*Habibi*, there I was tonight, driving into the neighborhood my dad always warned me not to visit. You ready for this one?" Danny is such a superb storyteller.

"I'm ready because you're alive, so I know it's a happy ending," I reply as we both laugh. From the corner of my eye, I catch Amira smiling flirtatiously at me but looking impatiently for my attention.

"Ashe, she's the love of my life. I knew it from the moment I met her."

"I'm happy for you. The best thing I've heard all day. But why does Miss Lebanon live in such a dangerous neighborhood?"

"*Habibi*, she is a Shite Muslim. That's where they live. The same way we live on the Christian side of Lebanon. They have their own side with their own militia, their own laws. It's like a different country. A Christian can go in and never come back out, and no police authority will dare to go search for the body."

"Dude, didn't you just warn me today the one rule not to break is to date outside of your religion? And you're clearly breaking it. For what? What's so worth risking your life?" I say, annoyed, raising my voice.

"Love. Love, *habibi*. I haven't felt this way in my whole life," he says quietly. "And it's not just my life. She's risking hers too. If she's caught with a Christian, she could be outcast by her own family. It's serious."

"That's heavy." His sentiment hits me in a deep place within my soul.

"Listen to this, when I picked her up today, she was standing six feet away from my car and I couldn't recognize her. She had an all-black burka on."

"I don't want to be disrespectful, but what's that?"

"The all-black gown that covers the entire body but her kohl-lined eyes," he explains as I remember seeing footage on American news from Iraq of women wearing head-to-toe black clothing with only their black-liner eyes showing.

"Holy shit! You're dating a girl that's wearing an all-black burka walking around this nightclub right now. I want to see her. Where is she?" I say teasingly.

"No, no, no. There's more." He laughs as he continues the story. "I called her and said, 'Where you at?' She answers the phone, 'Danny, I'm standing right in front of you. Hurry, before they notice.' And so I look up, and all I see is a pair of eyes just floating around the blackness. She hops in my car, and as we race away, she whips off her burka and has sexy nightclub clothes underneath. It was like we escaped together for love. It was such a turn-on."

"Look at you. I've never seen you so happy. Love has no religion. You'll remember this moment forever. Let's be good to it," I say, feeling his joyfulness.

"Thank you. I love that you're here with me. For once, let us be kings," Danny says, holding my shoulder. "We're bringing the biggest music act in the world to Beirut. There's no one hotter than 50 Cent right now. And it's the first time Lebanon has put on a concert like this. No one imagined it was possible, and we're going to do it. We're making history. I swear, everyone who is somebody wants to meet us. It's crazy."

"Talking about kings, look at the size of this bottle." They turn the music off and the enormous bottle of Cristal makes its appearance, grabbing the attention of every single person in the club.

"This must be some big baller, brother. How much do you think that bottle is?" I say to Danny, watching the numerous sparklers light the way toward us.

"That's a $75,000 bottle."

The DJ on a microphone chants "Amira, Amira" and the entire club follows suit as the sparkling bottle caravan heads to our coveted corner.

"Ashe, she wants to make sure she has your attention. We've been talking for too long," Danny says with a chuckle. "She wants you! She wouldn't do this for just anyone."

I turn toward Amira and see her stern, emotionless stare. I'm wondering what game she's up to. She knows I can't afford a bottle like this. I feel invisible golden handcuffs tightening on my wrists as she continues to stare at me, smiling now. I turn my back to look at the crowd beneath us. No woman has ever tamed me. She's going to learn the hard way that my freedom is worth more than her gold.

With a champagne glass in his hand, Danny asks if I was able to get a glass before the bottle was emptied within literally seconds by Amira's elite set. We laugh that I didn't even get a chance to find out what a $75,000 bottle of champagne tastes like. The music stops again and the sparkling caravan appears with the crowd chanting her name. She stands there in the middle of her huge VIP table, stoic, loving every minute of the spotlight. The shocked expression on my face brings her so much joy.

Now that the club is lit up by the sparklers, I notice a tall, striking familiar redhead making her way toward us from the bathroom.

"Hi, Michelle!" I say, surprised to see her again. "You're in Beirut?"

"Yeah, of course. I'm staying with you guys." She's holding a girl's hand who is standing behind her.

"Have you met Danny's girlfriend? I love her." Michelle pulls a stunning black-haired girl in front of me. Danny definitely has an eye for beautiful women. I notice her sultry, kohl-rimmed green eyes and subdued demeanor.

"Hi, I'm Sana."

HOUDINI'S ESCAPE

"Who needs a ship when you can fly... "

Walking up the spiraling stone staircase to Danny's chalet alone, I watch my first sunrise in the Middle East. It's a haunting thought to know the entire world looks at the same sun rising every day, yet humans cannot see eye to eye. So much war, suffering, division and not enough peace and empathy.

When I open the door, I find myself thrust into a busy office atmosphere. The maids are cleaning the bedrooms. Four Apple Macs are set up in the living room toward all the windows.

Abdul is sitting in front of his laptop, on the phone, facing the cedar mountains. Teddy is on the phone as well, speaking in Arabic, pacing back and forth and gesturing. It must be something important.

Michelle surprises me, walking out of the kitchen with coffee in her hand, wearing a wispy cornflower-blue slip dress and asking if I would like some breakfast. She leaves the coffee on the desk and goes back to the kitchen. Behind her, another familiar face walks out.

"Anwar! Oh my God! You're in Lebanon too?" I say and we hug. Another LA transplant, Anwar is one of Danny's partners and a lifelong friend. He is Lebanese Greek, with pale-olive skin, brown eyes and a big smile, and somewhere in his mid to late 30s. Anwar is a trusted friend who always gets jokes last, a little slow but with a warm heart.

"Of course, brother," he replies, laughing. "There's never a day without friends at Danny's."

"So true. The couch always has a reservation. By the way, have you guys seen him? I've been trying to reach him all morning."

"Oh, don't you worry about Danny. He said he had something important to do today."

I motion to the office set-up in the living room. "Wow, I wasn't expecting you guys to start work this early."

"Are you just coming back in from last night?" Abdul asks me as soon as he gets off the phone.

"Fortunately, yes," I reply slyly, trying to avoid more questions.

"Oh, this is Ashe, dude. There's always a story," Anwar says confidently.

"Wait, wait, wait. It's Erick Morillo's booking agent. One second, I want to hear all the tea," Abdul says, smiling, as he hurries back on his phone.

"Yo, Ashe, this computer is yours," Teddy says while covering the phone he's talking on with his hand and pointing to the laptop in the corner, facing the sea.

Settling at the snug corner desk, I see a list of what needs to be done on my part for today.

Anwar picks up the list. "I already did the first two. You just need to get the hotels covered and reserve the limos for these dates."

"Easy, I got you." I flick on the laptop and start searching for five-star hotels and limo services.

Abdul and Teddy get off their phones, looking at me expectantly.

"I heard you had a wild first night in Beirut," Teddy says, smirking.

"Oh, this is going to be good. This is about the crazy honking billionaire," Abdul says while stretching his back into the leather chair, and then he yells toward the kitchen, "Michelle, can you get me some tea?"

"PLEASE!" Anwar tells Abdul, who's clearly used to a fleet of servants in whatever Qatar palace he comes from.

"Yes, yes, please, Miss Michelle," he says in a polite voice.

Michelle sticks her head out from the kitchen door, her long flame-red hair glistening against the white wall. "'Course, honey. Anyone else want anything?"

"Dude, Michelle is such a sweetheart," Teddy says.

"Aww, thank you, boys," she says sweetly.

I stretch my arms behind my head. "I don't know what you want to hear, but it was an exciting night. We left the nightclub, and she made sure I came with her to some obscenely expensive hotel by the beach. Amira likes to party on another level. She paid for the entire floor for her friends to party with her and a penthouse suite overlooking the sea for the two of us. I've never partied so hard. And this brought out the most bizarre conversations I've ever had with a woman."

"C'mon, dude! Did you fuck her?" Anwar cuts me off anxiously, expecting a racier story.

I lean in, take a deep breath to pause as Abdul asks, "What type of conversations do you mean?"

The phone rings again. Teddy jumps up to answer and yells, "Hold that thought. It's the bank. Abdul, are you ready to transfer 55k to the business account?"

"Ashe, one second!" Abdul says as he rushes to log on to his laptop. He motions to Teddy, "I'm ready. Done."

"Great, I have the confirmation number. Erick Morillo signed and booked. Sixth beach party done," Teddy announces as he high-fives Abdul.

"Good job, boys. We have two more beach parties to go," Anwar says to them.

Abdul smiles, his hawkish eyes fixed on me. "Go on, Ashe."

They all turn their chairs to face me. I even notice Michelle leaning against the kitchen door frame, looking rapt.

I take a deep breath and continue, "I mean, I've met girls who want to buy a nice purse, a nice car, even a nice house.

Amira seems obsessed with status and wealth on a completely different level. She kept on talking about changing the value of the Lebanese currency in the global market. Amira doesn't give a fuck about anything you can buy for a million dollars. She cares about providing steel for high-rise hotels across Europe, and bringing the Ritz-Carlton to Beirut is the next deal she's working on. She literally believes she's a steward of Lebanon. Her last deal was the American military barracks for the ongoing war in Iraq."

Anwar laughs. "That's so funny you're dating a woman who cares so much about money, and you're the last person on this earth who does."

Abdul sits stunned, open-mouthed, forgetting to sip his tea as I continue, "In the evening's course, she kept on getting calls from various global government leaders. While partying, she was securing multimillion-dollar deals. I've seen nothing like it. Multitasking like an octopus on her three laptops. But that wasn't the most shocking part of the night."

"Oh, here we go! Here comes the part I've been waiting for," Anwar says, clapping his hands in excitement.

"You know, Ashe, it's unheard of for a woman in my culture to be allowed to handle business, let alone billions of her father's money," says Abdul. "Women in the Middle East are born to walk behind the man, not in front."

"I like Amira," Michelle says, "she's unique. So you guys like your women to be pretty, rich but silent, and power is just reserved for men? That's fucked up. I'm so glad I live in America."

"I love a powerful woman," I reply to Michelle, "but the demand of obedience and loyalty she commands is suffocating."

"Ashe, if she thinks she can break you in like a wild horse she's in for a rude awakening. I've seen so many women try, but you always seem to fly free, brother. You're a crazy motherfucker. If I could chill with a billionaire, that would be it. 'Call me on my yacht in Montenegro, bitch!'" Anwar says with sarcasm in his voice, and everybody laughs.

The front door slams open and Danny rushes in. "Let's go, boys, time to work," he says. "We have the biggest concert in Lebanon's history to pull off. I need Smirnoff on the phone. We need more marketing money."

"Thank God! I thought you got kidnapped," I say to him.

"That would be some crazy shit." Danny laughs and turns to the others. "Boys, I don't know what Ashe did to Amira last night, but she has been calling me all morning thanking me for the best sex she's ever had in her life."

Danny chuckles as everyone else stares at me, stunned.

Michelle pops her head out of the kitchen again. "I've heard the same thing from so many of my friends. Jesus, Ashe! What do you do to these girls?"

In his ADD way, Danny swiftly changes the subject. "But for real, guys, I just finished a meeting with my dad and the other generals. Your boy, DB, got the best security for the 50 Cent concert. Check it out. A swarm of army troops with a battle tank to secure the venue. Ever heard of that? The most amazing security in the world. We'll be on the news for that too," he adds, looking pleased with himself. "Now let's focus on these side hustles. How are the beach parties coming along? You know we can pull an extra million on those."

Our team quickly shifts into work mode again.

The speed of the days passes us by with many meetings, staffing, press calls, radio interviews, hotel and private plane bookings and setting up ticket distribution for the concert. All this is happening between late nights at Beirut's hottest night-clubs, where they treat us like celebrities. Everyone knows us as "the Americans" bringing the biggest rapper in the world to Beirut. Sheiks, politicians, high-ranked military officials, the head of the US Embassy in Beirut, the list goes on.

One afternoon a few weeks in, my phone rings. As always, it's Amira, who has been a reoccurring theme in my days since we met.

"I'm downstairs, let's go," she demands. "I have a surprise."

Danny overhears her loud voice and tells me, "You gotta go."

"I'll be downstairs in a minute," I reply as I hang up.

"*Habibi*, don't forget to mention the beach parties. She can still invest."

"I got you," I say as I close the door behind me, sprinting down the stairs. In a rush, I forget my phone on my desk.

Today she is driving a lime-green Lamborghini. Her vivid green Prada dress and shoes match the car. As always, she looks flawless, like she stepped out of a glossy magazine.

"Which one did you buy first, the car or the dress?" I tease her as I get into her sports car.

"Shooo, Ashe. Don't make me smile too much. You'll give me wrinkles."

"At least I'll give you something your money can't buy," I reply sarcastically.

Amira breaks into a hard laugh and slams her foot as a reflex on the accelerator. As we speed away, I notice, for the first time, a giant white statue high up, looming over Jounieh from the cedar-cloaked mountains.

"What is that?" I ask, pointing to the statue.

"Oh, that's Harissa. The Virgin Mary."

Mesmerized by the gigantic white statue sparkling from the backdrop of the greenery of the cedars, I make the sign of the Holy Cross in respect.

"*Really?!*" Amira says to me with a bit of disgust. "Wow, you drink that Kool-Aid, huh?"

Stunned, with my head still in a bow, I ask, "What do you mean?"

"Oh, honey. Don't you know? Religion is for the masses. It's only here to control you," she replies with conviction as we drive, looping around closer to the coast now.

"Interesting. I don't feel controlled. I feel closer to something bigger than myself."

"Closer? To what? God?" She breaks out in a deep, throaty laugh. "There's no God, honey. You're a grown-ass man still believing in Santa Claus. Like there's someone in the clouds with a long white beard? Surely you can't be fooled this easily."

"Fooled? If not for my mother's faith, I wouldn't even be here," I reply, shaken.

"Explain, let me hear it."

"My mother has sickle-cell disease. When she got pregnant with me, the doctors told her to have an abortion because the childbearing would be a death sentence for both of us. She refused because of her absolute faith in God, saying that as long as God is willing and the child in her womb is fighting to survive, so will she—"

"Yes, yes, enough," she cuts me off dismissively, changing the vibe. "Look at this box at your feet."

Stunned by her rudeness, I glance down at a small green box on the passenger-side floor. "That's for you, honey. Happy one-month anniversary. You need to look presentable. Mentioning mothers, you're about to meet mine. Enough of this religion dogma stuff. You'll embarrass yourself."

She seems irritated as we pull in to the port's valet. A large, at least 150-foot yacht with four decks and two helicopter pads is docked in front of us. I open the box. It's an 18k yellow-gold presidential Rolex watch. Amira smiles at my surprised reaction.

"I can't accept this." I hand the box back to her.

"Don't be silly." She puts the watch on my wrist, carelessly throwing the empty box on the car floor for someone else to pick up. "There, now you look like we belong together."

Hesitantly, I get out of the Lamborghini and notice the crew dressed in all white ushering us onto this massive boat.

The young captain greets us as we board and takes us through the yacht to the circular dining area. Sitting at the mahogany table are Amira's brother, sister and mother, impatiently awaiting our arrival.

"Finally! This is the man I've heard so much about," her mother says, extending her bejeweled hand. Her smile somehow detaches from the expression in her dark eyes, which seems to be completely the opposite. Being two-faced is an acquired trait of the rich.

"It's a nice surprise to meet you." I reach down to shake her hand, uncomfortably smiling at Amira as she introduces me to her brother and sister. They both acknowledge me and we sit down for lunch.

The air is thick with tension as we sit in silence at the table. Amira sits next to her mother and tells the captain to sail around the harbor. The boat becomes alive with the crew moving around, serving us caviar, lobster and champagne as we cast off.

"So you are the American who is bringing this big musician to Beirut. All my girlfriends are talking about it," Amira's mother says to me politely but with an interrogative glance.

"It's actually my best friend's company. I'm just here to assist."

"I know, that's what I've heard," she replies, as I realize it was a trick question. She was trying to see if I would inflate my importance to impress her.

"Stop, Mom!" Amira says, her cheeks flushing red through her makeup. "I invited him to enjoy lunch with us. No more questions, please."

I'm surprised at the bullish way Amira takes control of the atmosphere, and everyone just goes along. The mood turns more polite as the conversation shifts over to her sister's college choices in the United States. The absence of her brother's input to the conversation is noticeable. He just sits, eats and stares at the sea. Now that I see this family's dynamic, I understand why Amira is the boss of her father's company.

After finishing lunch, her mother says, "So, you've been spending so much time with my daughter. Are you planning on staying in Beirut after the concert?"

"I'm not sure. Why?"

"Well, she seems to be very fond of you. I have never seen my daughter spend so much time with any boy," she says awkwardly, smiling.

"Shush, Mom." Amira tries to cut her off as they argue in Arabic, making me feel uncomfortable.

The saving grace is her kind sister motioning me to come up on the deck to enjoy the scenery of Jounieh's Harbor. After shouting at each other, Amira and her mother follow us to the deck a few minutes later.

Amira takes my hand and pulls me aside. "Don't let my mother get to you. She's just protective of me."

"Protective of you?" I laugh. "What's she scared of? That I'll get you pregnant and we'll get married?"

"That's funny, honey. Just because I would be pregnant with your baby doesn't mean I'd marry you," she replies, laughing.

"Wait, what? So you're telling me that if you were pregnant and I got down on one knee and asked you to marry me, you'd say no?"

"Of course I'd say no. Marriage is a business deal. And what do you bring to the table? Love? It's a lose-lose situation for me. The only thing I can gain is a pretty baby who I would have to take care of," she says in an unforgiving tone.

The veil is lifted. For the first time, I can see clearly why my heart just could not fall for Amira.

"You're right," I say but with a weird sense of relief. I look out and notice that we are only 300 yards from the shore. Suddenly, I spot Danny's chalet in the far distance and smile back at Amira with a thought. With the red sun setting at my back, I hand her the Rolex. "This watch belongs to someone else. I need to be needed. What I'm looking for isn't here."

Her ghostly brown eyes stare at me without any sign of emotion as she clutches the Rolex tightly in her hand.

Without warning, my soul compels my body to dive from the third deck into the turquoise waters of the Mediterranean.

I leap into the surf. The water hugs my body with warmth, as I only have shorts and a light polo shirt on. Under the water, my leather sandals sink to the bottom of the sea. As I swim away toward the city, which is now lighting up in the dusk, I hear their voices shouting incoherently.

Standing disturbed, now with her entire family leaning against the deck's railing, Amira is frantically waving for me to come back. But as she screams, she can only watch me disappear, like a magician, from her golden clutches.

BLONDE DIAMOND

"Harrisa's songbird"

Each step out of the salty crystal-blue waters feels like a shackle breaking on the large stone boulders. Coming out of the sea, I feel like I've made it to the promised land. No phone, no wallet, no shoes and exhausted from the swim to my deliverance. I lie on the rocky shore, stretched on my back, watching Amira's yacht disappear on the reddening horizon and listening to the city come alive with the pounding waves at my feet. Well, that was one way of ending a relationship: jumping into the sea to escape.

I hear distant screams of excitement and honking cars, and loud music drifting out from neighboring restaurants. The music reminds me that I am again free and single in this mystical land. The excitement envelops me as I think of going out tonight with my boys for the first time unattached. As my eyes wander along the sunset skies, I really start feeling what Danny has been saying: "We will be kings."

I get up and walk toward Danny's chalet. No one notices me. It's a beautiful feeling to be a fly on the wall for once. Cars speed past with passengers holding Italian, German, French, Brazilian and Spanish flags.

I notice a soccer game on all the TV screens as I walk past these venues, packed with people screaming: "GOOOOOOOAAALL!!!"

Wow, it's the World Cup. I forgot it was today, but it's on the hearts and lips of everyone I'm passing by. Maybe that's why no one notices the barefooted and soaking-wet refugee who came out of the sea. Smiling at every passing face, I feel so light, like I'm flying. The cobblestone streets are so smooth they are slippery under my wet feet. Walking along the shore side of Jounieh, the smell of the sea and the people's enthusiasm feel like an island carnival. In front of me, I see a huge projector screen in the outdoor dining area of one of my favorite restaurants, Bread and Brown. Inching closer, I hear someone shouting my name. It's the owner, Marco, waving me in. "Ashe, Ashe!"

"Hey, Marco!" I reply as I try to just walk by and hurry to the chalet. His face shifts from friendliness to bewilderment when he notices my soaking clothes. His outstretched arms, ready for his usual welcoming embrace, drop when I get closer to him.

"What is this?" He points to my wet clothes, laughing. "Did it rain and I missed it?"

"If I told you, you wouldn't believe me."

"Ah, you crazy Americans. Come, come. You are shivering. I get you some hot tea and a towel." He pats me on the back as he steers me toward the only open table. "Please, please."

I try to resist. "I have no money. I forgot my wallet and my phone at the chalet."

"Aaaah, one of those days. My friend, don't worry. I know the owner." He puts his hand on his chest and laughs again as he slides the chair out for me. This type of kindness the Lebanese people display to a stranger is not something I've ever experienced in my life. I can feel that their incredible warmth and sense of values are changing me.

"Thank you. I really appreciate you. Please, just start a tab for me. I'll pay for it tomorrow," I reply, sitting down at the table.

He taps me on my shoulder again and mumbles in Arabic to the server. He smiles at me and hurries inside the packed restaurant. As his robust figure moves away from my sight, it reveals a silhouette of a young woman sitting across from me. Three friends surround her at the table, as she is gracefully sipping on her pink drink. She seems to be out of place and time. There is a sophisticated gentleness about her. She looks like Grace Kelly. She has a palomino's mane of pale-blonde hair, shiny and thick, falling in waves around her face and down past her waist, a rare sight in this part of the world. She is the first blonde I've seen in Lebanon. If not for her friends, who are clearly speaking in Arabic to her, I would assume she was a tourist. She reminds me of California. She must feel me staring at her because her glance meets mine.

Her hazel eyes look at me as if she has known me her whole life, and in that moment, everyone else disappears. Those seconds feel like an eternity. Looking at her, I feel as though we are speaking in a dead language without words.

Interrupting this magical moment, the server shows up with my tea. "Can I get you anything else, sir Ashe?" he asks among the ear-splitting chatter and laughter.

"As a matter of fact, yes. What's that pink drink the blonde girl is drinking?" I ask in a half-whisper.

"Oh, that is our special strawberry smoothie," he whispers back. "It's trendy."

"Lemme put one on my tab, please, and send it over to her."

"Very good, sir."

I can't stop looking at her. I haven't been this nervous in a long time. What am I doing? I was just embracing my new independence again and imagining what I could do with it in this sleepless city. Rarely do I hit on women. The need to pursue connections is not there. They just come into my life unexpectedly. I believe there are no coincidences. When relationships come, they are gifts from the universe. Every relationship in my life has been a lesson, whether good or bad.

I am so out of my comfort zone with no friends to break the ice or give an introduction. With my soaking-wet clothes and bare feet, my appearance is farcical while hers is classy. She is wearing a long white skirt with a nude fitted top and a large buckle belt that accentuates her fit figure. Her bronzed skin makes her pale-gold hair stand out even more.

The server hurries through the crowd, holding her whipped-cream strawberry smoothie. Watching him deliver the drink, I can't even breathe. I'm so anxious, knowing that the blonde girl will look at me in a few seconds, and I will have to do something. I've undertaken an introduction I'm too scared to finish.

The server points over his left shoulder at me as he briefly talks to her before walking away. This time, our eyes make contact, but she acknowledges me with a slight nod. Her friends smile more obviously and wave me over to their table. When you sky dive, there is no getting back on the plane after you jump. So I leap out of my seat.

Her friends all start talking to me in Arabic and I feel her silently watching me.

"I'm sorry, I don't speak Arabic," I say, sitting down on the chair they offer.

"Shoooo, Americani?!" her male friend asks, surprised, with his arm around a girl with long dark hair.

"Yes, I'm American."

"Really? You look a little Lebanese," the dark-haired girl says.

"Actually, I'm Colombian, Chinese, Dutch, Spanish, Caribbean and Lebanese on my father's side. My grandfather left Lebanon during the civil war and started a family in Colombia. I'm the first in my family to visit Lebanon since his departure."

"Wow, you're like the whole world," she says, and they all start laughing, and I notice the blonde has a sparkle in her smile.

"What's your name?" one of the two guys asks.

I turn to the blonde and extend my hand and say, "My name's Ashe. It's a pleasure to meet you."

She looks at her friends and then back at me. "My name is Aleyna. It's a pleasure to meet you as well." She shakes my hand gently and gives me a confident smile. "These are my friends, Carla, Cyril and George."

"It's a pleasure!" I say, shaking their hands.

"What are you doing in Lebanon, Ashe?" George, who is sitting to her left, asks me. "It's very dangerous for an American to be in the Middle East right now."

"I'm here with my best friend, Danny, who's from Jounieh. He's organizing a concert in Beirut this summer."

"Oh, you are the Americans with the 50 Cent concert?"

"Yeah, that's us."

Everyone at the table looks impressed. Aleyna, in her calm way, shifts the energy. "No shoes, no watch, wet? Let me guess... California?" She smiles, and I notice a sparkle in her smile again. I laugh, surprised by her wit.

"Since you already know who I am and where I'm from, satisfy my curiosity. Is that a diamond in your tooth?"

The table erupts in laughter again. They chatter some Arabic to Aleyna as George scoots his chair a few inches away to give her the stage.

"It is. So why are you wet? Did you just swim here from California?" Aleyna says with another smile showcasing her diamond.

Her friends all break into another burst of loud laughter. Carla is laughing hysterically and mumbling to Cyril in Arabic. All eyes are looking at me for a reply as Aleyna just sits there with a slight smile.

"Yes, to meet you," I say boldly. "It was worth it."

"Ha! Answer me this, Ashe from California. Why did you buy me this drink? What is it you want?" She goes straight for the jugular as she shifts her weight in the chair to the other side.

"I'm wet and freezing and your table was closer to the fire pit."

George and Cyril clap.

"Ahhhh, Americani. I like!" George says to Cyril while Carla looks at Aleyna with an uncertain expression.

"Just kidding, I had an extraordinary day," I say, pointing to my wet clothes. They all get seriously quiet, leaning in for my next words. "I'm not sure if you believe in angels, but something guided me here against all odds. This is the last place I'm supposed to be right now. If I didn't follow my heart, I wouldn't be sitting here with you. What do I want? Nothing, your smile is enough. It's an unexpected gift at the end of this torturous day."

Aleyna bites her lip. "And now that you've met me, what are you going to do?" She glances for a second at an older muscular man in a black suit a couple of tables away. She looks at Carla for a split second.

"Boys, it's too hot at this table and it's getting late. Let's go. *Yallah*," Carla says to George and Cyril.

"It was a pleasure meeting you, Ashe," George says to me as they all rise to leave.

"Yes, Ashe. Hopefully we see you again, my friend!" Cyril says, patting me on my wet back.

Aleyna stays behind while her friends wait for her outside the restaurant. She quickly glances at the muscular man again. "So, do you have an answer to my question?"

"To be honest, I've been in Lebanon for a short while and have only seen your wild nightlife. I would like to see Lebanon from a different perspective. If you'd be so kind, through your alluring eyes," I reply, looking into her hazel eyes that gleam in the firelight as much as her diamond-studded smile.

Suddenly the crowd leaps to their feet, cheering for a final goal that wins the game. Everyone is hugging and laughing. But for us, time stands still. Only us, two souls trapped in a motionless moment, overpowered by the feelings rising between us.

The sea breeze tangles her long honey-blonde hair in front of her face. "Have you seen Harissa?" she asks.

MY ENCHANTRESS'S FLUTE

"Which are you hearing: the words or the song?"

The waves of the Mediterranean brush softly against the large grey-stone boulders at the shore beneath my window. Most mornings, I wake to the sun streaming in and the sounds of seabirds and waves lapping the shore. It calms my anxious heart, excited to see her dazzling hazel eyes today. As the sun rises in the east, Abdul, my roommate, lays out his small red rug on the floor and gets on his knees to pray. His Muslim faith calls on him to do it five times a day. What an admirable dedication to his God. When I was young, kneeling at the edge of my bed, I remember making the sign of the cross and saying *The Lord's Prayer* before going to sleep. I don't do it anymore. Am I getting further from God, or does He pull me closer to Him in this ancient land?

Still half-asleep and groggy, I stumble my way to the kitchen as the maids clean my room. Danny, bright and wide-eyed, is brewing Arabic coffee, which is like Turkish coffee, for everybody.

"What did I say to you, *habibi*? I warned you not to break Amira's heart," he tells me in a concerned but gentle voice. "It's going to be hard for you to be in Lebanon now. She knows everyone. No girl is going to touch you after her. They're all afraid of her wrath."

"It all happened so fast, Danny, and all I could hear was my heart telling me it wasn't right. And I was right. I met a girl of a different kind last night."

"You American gypsy." He burst out laughing. "When will you settle down? Amira could've provided an incredible life for you here."

"My idea of an incredible life only requires the one thing money can't buy: love."

Danny places a cup of coffee in front of me. "I get it. Love. I'm risking my life every day for love. Every time I pick Sana up, I fear for our lives. But the way she makes me feel is worth everything. English is my third language. When I was in relationships with American women, I felt misunderstood because I couldn't always find the right words, but with Sana I can speak in my native tongue. She just gets me. It's what I've always yearned for."

I look into his eyes and see an emotion that men usually hide from one another. It's the first time I've seen it in Danny.

"Being here is changing us. Must be something in the air," I reply, looking out to the cedar mountains.

"Must be. I'm glad you're here with me."

"Me too, Danny. I have to take a shower and get ready to see this new girl. The journey continues."

Danny, shaking his head, says, "At least bring her and meet up with Sana and me later on. I have a surprise for you."

"If I can, will do."

It's a few minutes before noon and I'm standing in front of the Bread and Brown, where she told me to meet her. I'm always late but today I couldn't find anything more important to do than see this gentle honey-haired, hazel-eyed beauty again. I feel like a kid, worrying and wondering if she'll show up. I should have known when she refused to give me her phone number. I don't even know what car she drives, so I'm nervously looking into all the passing cars.

Twelve o'clock. I knew it! From the beginning, it was always too good to be true. Just as I turn around to head back home, I hear my name.

"Ashe!" Aleyna says from the rolled-down tinted window of her grey BMW X5. "Are you waiting for someone?"

"Aleyna, I've been waiting for someone my whole life. Could you be her?" I reply flirtatiously.

"Well?" she says with a cheeky smile as the passenger door unlocks. "Are you going to get in?"

"Depends on the destination, beautiful."

"Oh, Ashe. Don't focus on the destination, you'll lose sight of what's truly important." She opens the passenger door, revealing a beach towel draped across the seat. I get in.

"What's this towel for?"

"I didn't know if being wet is part of your sexy Californian motif," she replies with a smile and shrug of her tan shoulders. "I didn't want you to ruin my leather seat."

We both laugh as she gently speeds up and away from the city. We drive for some time, listening to her melodic house music, daydreaming of a life together.

The northern coastline, filled with small cute restaurants and picturesque beach houses, whizzes past. She glances over at me, her honey-blonde hair flowing in the breeze from the open window, her hazel eyes sparkling in the light. "Just so you know, I've never done this."

"I'm confused. We've done nothing," I reply, partially sarcastic and partially flirtatious.

"But I have. I've risked my honor by picking up a stranger because of the way he makes me feel."

"It's okay. I understand and appreciate your courage. Guess that makes two of us. I'm here allowing myself to feel something I've never felt before."

She smiles at me, rolling her eyes, as we pull into a cul-de-sac with a scattering of tiny beachfront restaurants and cafés.

"I'm positive you've said that before, likely multiple times. Okay, I hope you're hungry because we're here, Ashe." She gets out of her BMW and starts walking toward a small establishment.

"Wait? Is that a restaurant?"

"You wanted to see Lebanon through my eyes, right?" she says, gesturing toward the pretty beach houses and tiny cafés. "This place has been family owned and operated for at least 30 years, and the owner still wakes up every morning at 4 A.M. to make fresh bread for the best sandwiches you'll ever have."

"Sounds good."

Only the smells of the salty sea air and manakish, hot flatbreads with cheese and thyme, fill the air. She waves me in as we walk under the awning through the glass doors into the little café overlooking the sea. Sitting down at one of their seven tables, we watch the water lapping the shore. The ambiance is light and homey but romantic. The owner is very appreciative and knows her name as she orders fresh mint lemonades and two shawarmas, a sort of flatbread wrap, for both of us. I notice she's dressed in something that you would find in a Ralph Lauren catalogue. She has the sexy chic vibe down to a science. White shorts, Gucci sandals and a baby-blue fitted blouse accessorized with a tiny gold cross and delicate strands of pendants. With the greeny-blue of the sea in her background and the gauzy light illuminating her long gold hair, she looks like a fairy. All she needs is wings.

"I know this probably isn't what you were expecting."

"I wasn't expecting anything, and this and you are just perfect. By the way, I was just thinking, what's it like to be the only natural blonde in Lebanon?"

She sweeps her hair behind her right ear and looks straight into my eyes. "I'm not the only one, but since you brought it up,

I'm half-German and half-Lebanese. I speak German, Arabic and English. Do you speak any other languages?"

"You're mixed like me, and I find that incredibly beautiful that two cultures, worlds apart, are expressed inside you. And it so happens I also speak Spanish," I reply as the owner brings our food, which looks and smells delicious. I notice him dropping off food for a sturdy man sitting alone to the left of us who looks strangely familiar.

"Mmm, this is my favorite!" Aleyna says with her tooth diamond sparkling as she takes a big bite of her shawarma.

"Wow. Your company and this sandwich are beyond belief. I'm cherishing every second."

It's a strange emotion as we look at each other. I'm not planning what to say next, but every word just seems to fall into the right place and at the right time. There are these long pauses in our conversation, and we just look at each other in a comfortable silence.

With the sun in her eyes, she says it's time to go explore her country.

This time we drive back to Jounieh and park her car. She takes me to a little red cable car, and up and up to the top of the cedar mountains we go. The ride is mesmerizing and even more so because she is my guide. After our flight above the cedars, I can see exactly where we are going. It's hard to miss and hard to forget a giant white Virgin Mary statue, soaring out of the cedars with her head tilted to the side and her protective arms outstretched toward Beirut.

Along the way, after lighting our white candles, I see a man in a simple tattered robe sitting against the wall with a wooden reed-like object in his lap. Aleyna walks up to him and gives him some money. He smiles and picks up the stick, starts playing a wistful otherworldly tune. I realize that the stick is an instrument I've never heard before but am unlikely to forget anytime soon.

"What an enchanting sound. What instrument is that?" I ask Aleyna as we continue walking with even more magic in the air thanks to the street musician.

"He's playing the ney flute." She closes her eyes and moves slowly with her hands open, like a dancer in the wind.

"This sound belongs on this mountain. It resonates deep inside me," I say to her, feeling the goosebumps on my arms.

"Yes, you can feel the ney in your soul because it's been around for 5,000 years. Even before your first time hearing it, you still feel like somehow you already know it."

Once we near the top, I ask her, "Do you believe in past lives?"

"Ashe, can I be honest with you? I believe I knew you the moment I saw you. That's why I am excited we're here." She leads me up to the top of the shrine and all I can see are her glowing eyes reflecting the entire landscape of Lebanon. Her perfume is light and earthy, and her walk is soft but confident. Every time she smiles at me, I realize I'm grinning.

"This is Harissa," she says as we stop at the feet of Our Lady of Lebanon.

Seeing the glistening city and the deep-blue sea on the horizon, I turn to her. "There're only a few moments in life you truly never forget. This is one of them for me. Thank you."

"I've brought no one up here before, but I just felt you were the one," she says as we both slowly lean in toward each other.

My arms wrap around her tiny waist, and as I embrace her, I can feel my heart pounding wildly.

Looking up at me with her hazel eyes and red lips parted, she puts her right hand on my chest and whispers, "Are you ready to open your heart or is it broken?"

"Aleyna, since I've met you, my heart has been free and open."

"Then kiss me."

Our lips seal together in a fiery kiss. With a wispy breeze, the woodsy smell of the cedar trees and the sound of the ney playing, time disappears.

"That felt like lightning," I whisper in her ear.

"I feel the same. We've been thunderstruck."

I hold her closer to my chest as she tucks her head under my chin and wraps her arms around my back.

The ney player stops suddenly, and I open my eyes.

Holy fuck! I instantaneously feel all the blood rushing through my entire body.

The sturdy man in the blue suit and dark sunglasses is glaring straight at me, with an evil vehemence. Mephistopheles in human flesh. And I see he's armed. *Fuck, fuck, fuck!* Now I remember, he was there at Bread and Brown when I first met

Aleyna and there again at the beachfront restaurant earlier. How did I miss that he's been following us this whole time?

Danny warned me this could happen in Beirut.

CARELESS SECRET

"Fear came to whisper lies."

Mephistopheles in the blue suit and dark shades has spun me out of the most magical moment I've ever had. Not even the holiness of this shrine deters this demon. My first thought is to protect Aleyna, but I can't tell her. Her fear might make things worse. I need to get us out of here safely as soon as possible. Mephistopheles notices my gaze back at him and turns around, pretending he has no business with me.

I can't hesitate, this is my chance to get us out of here. I see the last passengers getting off the red cable car as it's about to board for the ride down. I pull along a surprised Aleyna, and we swiftly make our way to the red cable car. Her questions about what's wrong go unanswered. But we make it to the cable car in time for the doors to close behind us, as I see Mephistopheles chasing me. I sigh with relief as the cable car moves down and he's left behind on the platform.

"Ashe, answer me. What happened up there? Did I do something wrong?" Aleyna demands, shaken by my odd behavior.

It's a struggle to find words that are not a lie. I don't want to ruin a pure feeling between us with dishonesty, but how do I tell her our lives are in danger because of me?

High in the air, soaring over the treetops, I hold her hands and look into her beautiful eyes. "You absolutely did nothing wrong. There is a..." Suddenly my phone rings before I'm able to finish the sentence. It's Danny.

"Ashe, *habibi*, I've been trying to reach you. We're waiting for you. Let me give you the address," he says in a hurry.

I repeat the address out loud to Aleyna. She nods, confirming she knows the destination.

"Okay, Danny, as soon as we get to the car, we will be on our way," I reply, relieved to know that we will soon be far away from Mephistopheles and in Danny's safe company.

"Aleyna, I'm not sure what this address is to, but my friend invited us to some sort of surprise. I'd love if you come with me," I say to her, holding her closely coming down the mountain as I look behind us for Mephistopheles.

"Ashe, only if you promise not to rush through these precious moments we have together," she replies when we get off the cable car and start walking briskly to her car.

"Look, I'll be honest with you. Up there, I saw an armed man, who I'm certain has been following me since yesterday.

I didn't want to scare you, but Danny warned me that as an American, I should be careful in Beirut."

She looks behind us up the mountain as we get into the car. "What did this man look like?"

"Dunno. He's a big guy, with a shaved head, in a blue suit. And he had a gun. But don't worry, I made sure we left him up there."

"It's going to be okay, Ashe. Don't worry." She seems utterly unfazed. "I need to make a quick phone call. Wait here."

She gets out of the car and has a conversation with someone in Arabic for maybe half a minute. This is so surreal. My head is on a swivel in her car, looking around for Mephistopheles to pop out from any corner to abduct me, and here she is, casually making a phone call. When she hangs up the phone, she sits back in the driver's seat, fastens her seatbelt and gives me a smile. Her calm demeanor makes me more nervous. She finally starts the car and slowly takes off toward the city.

Driving down the southern coast of Lebanon, the bustling city and cars of Beirut disappear. The sapphire sea on our right-hand side glistens to the beat of her chill house music as my eyes are still glued to the side mirror. Arriving at the address Danny provided us, we see a Tahitian utopia in the middle of nowhere.

"I don't mean to be rude, but is this the address? What is this?" I ask when we pull into the sandy parking lot.

"Yeah. That's it," she says confidently but also looking surprised.

I call Danny to notify him of our arrival.

"*Habibi*, are you here?" he asks happily.

"Yes, Danny. I'm in the middle of nowhere, not sure if this is it? I'm by the sea at a place that looks like Tahiti meets the Sahara Desert."

"Oh yeah, you're here. I'm coming," he says decidedly and hangs up.

I look at Aleyna, who sweetly shrugs and takes my hand with a big smile. "I guess today's filled with adventures."

"I welcome the color of your life into my gray background. It's pretty intoxicating."

Holding hands, we walk toward the grand entrance. I cautiously scan the road for any suspicious cars that may have followed us. Danny greets us from the enormous dark-oak doors.

"Surprise," he shouts as I give him a hug and introduce Aleyna to my best friend.

Walking past two giant wooden tiki statues, I ask, "What is this place?"

"What is this place is not as surprising as whose is this place," Danny replies, smiling as I notice our good old friend Johnny rounding the corner. He is a talented contractor, an ex-Hollywood promoter who's half Lebanese and grew up with me in LA.

"Surprise, motherfucker!" Johnny shouts and picks me up in a bear hug.

"Johnny! Whadda hell are you doing here?"

"You're looking at it! This is my place. I sold my house and business in LA and built this. Welcome, brother. And who is this beautiful lady with you?"

Aleyna, still clasping my hand, steps in shyly from behind me.

"This is Aleyna, my girl."

She squeezes my hand and looks into my eyes with a gratified but astounded expression as I introduce my friends to her. I feel assured for now that she accepted my label for our quickly blossoming relationship.

"Lemme show you guys around my water oasis," Johnny says, too excited to waste any time. He walks us around his enormous resort filled with restaurants playing a World Cup match on the big plasma TVs, two Olympic-size pools, cabanas on the beachfront and new villas under construction.

"Wow, Johnny, you've really outdone yourself, brother. This place is sick."

Smiling with pride, he whisks us to the beachfront part of the resort, spilling out onto the shore with a wooden deck bar, laid out with elegant modular sofas, retro deck chairs and a DJ spinning. We stop at the beachfront restaurant, done up with Persian rugs and vintage photographs of surfers, where a table is waiting for us to watch the sunset. Beneath the glowing Edison lights, I spot Sana waiting for us at the dark wooden table. I introduce the girls to each other. Johnny leaves to take care of business while the rest of us sit down for an early dinner.

As usual, Danny is the center of attention. "Whoa, you guys look beautiful together. Look at you, which designer runway did you walk off?"

Blushing, both Aleyna and I laugh it off. Sana also finds this hilarious, as she does anything that Danny says.

"Ashe, can you believe Johnny built all this? What a life he made for himself here. I think we can make it big in Lebanon," Danny says to me while we're all staring at a beautiful sunset. "I don't know if I wanna go back to the US after this concert."

"I know that look. What are you thinking?" I reply, seeing that his brain has already computed the next step in his life.

"Well, *habibi*, I have another big surprise for you!" He smirks and dances in his chair to the beat of the music playing in the background. I have a flashback to when we were making a deal with Alex that resulted in us being here.

"Oh, here it comes... the genie is about to come out of the lamp!" I giggle and clap my hands, turning toward the girls, who look eager to hear what Danny is about to say.

"Look at this. We can't do this in LA," he says, gesturing around him. "Today we sold out all the tickets for 50 Cent, and Alex called congratulating us, asking who's next. We can be the bridge between the biggest artists in the world and Lebanon. No one else has ever pulled this off. Plus, I'm in love and the sky is the limit here. I think I'm staying." He gives Sana a kiss and she happily tears up to the sound of his words.

"That's amazing, Danny. Congrats!" I say, noticing Aleyna's gaze drift from me to the red-gold sun slowly melting into the sea.

"Don't congratulate me because you're a big part of this, and I really want you to stay with me. I need your help in choosing blockbuster artists to follow this concert and keep growing our brand. Any ideas?"

"I'd get Shakira next."

Aleyna and Sana both shout at the same time, "She's half Lebanese!"

"Oh my God, Ashe. I would've never thought of her. She would kill it here, and she has never performed in Lebanon," Danny replies excitedly and clinks his margarita against my cocktail glass. "That's why my best friend is my most trusted business advisor."

The girls laugh and clap.

I take a sip of my piña colada and say, "I'm happy for you, but I have to say I don't know how I feel about staying here. I don't speak Arabic, I don't have family here and I constantly stick out like a tourist in this culture. Plus, I didn't tell you yet, but I almost got kidnapped just about an hour ago, while minding my own business on a date with my girl," I reply, changing the mood at the table.

Aleyna takes my hand. "Ashe—"

"No, no," I interrupt her. "This is Danny, my best friend. I have to tell him."

"Are you sure someone was going to kidnap you? Maybe you've seen too many American movies," Danny says calmly while Sana giggles.

Aleyna tries to stop me. "Ashe—"

"Yes, I'm positive. The guy was following me since yesterday, and he had a gun! There's no way that this big guy, by coincidence, is eating at the beach at the same restaurant and then takes a stroll at Harissa at the same time I'm there. And then chases me down to the cable car!"

Sana laughs. "It's funny to see an American afraid of one little man with a tiny gun."

"He wasn't little and it wasn't a tiny—"

"C'mon, Ashe," Danny cuts me off, "you've never seen a dude with a gun? You're from LA, brother. How many gang-bangers you see with guns all the time? Don't let this dude scare you. Do you see drive-by shootings on the news every night in Beirut? Trust me, this city is safer than LA."

"Ashe, I really have to get going," Aleyna says quietly to me as she looks at her cellphone ringing.

My heart sinks, thinking of a moment without her.

"Let's celebrate tonight at Crystal!" Danny yells out, changing the subject, dismissive of my concerns.

"Yes, perfect, Danny. I have to go home to change," Sana says with excitement. She, like Danny, loves to party and they seem made for each other.

"No worries, love. I'll drop you off," Danny replies to her as she smiles back at him.

"I'll be right back. Let me walk Aleyna to her car," I say to them as I take her warm hand and lead her toward the exit on the beach.

As the sun is disappearing, we walk slowly, and in silence, still holding hands. I see in her eyes both of our words that have gone unspoken.

"Is there something wrong?" I ask her as we near her car,

but she only glances at me and then back at the red horizon. We make it safely to her BMW and I put my hands around her waist. "This is one of those incredible days I never want to end. Please be my guest tonight. Come with us to Crystal."

She lays her hand on my face. "Was it really a magical day, or am I just another girl to you?"

I pull her closer to me, and our foreheads tilt to touch. Looking into her sparkly brown eyes, I say, "My heart has been dancing with you in the sun all day. Please let's continue this dream in the moonlight, tonight."

She grazes my lips with hers. "I see a dragon that wants to be tamed. See you again tonight, before you vanish, my wet Californian. I'll be there at 11."

I open the car door for her. She slips into the driver's seat, shoots me a kind smile, and disappears slowly, driving away in a sand cloud.

Suddenly, a car zips by, missing me by mere inches, and in that instant, I see Mephistopheles behind the wheel following into a sandy cloud. I panic. *Fuck!* I realize I still don't have her phone number. Some primal instinct takes over my body and I run after her. Sprinting as fast as I can, waving my hands to signal her to stop, but she's already gone.

SLIVER OF OMNISCIENCE

"Even in the dark, everything comes to light with the moon."

As Danny races back to the city in his BMW, I fix my eyes on the road, looking for any signs of Aleyna. *Was this our last goodbye? The last time I see her? Is she safe? I'd never forgive myself if something happened to her.* These thoughts race in my head as I search for a familiar shadow on the road.

"*Habibi*, she's okay! Stop worrying," Danny snaps me out of my dark thoughts as he gazes back at me. "You've been silent this whole time."

I meet his eyes in the rearview mirror without saying a word.

"Really? C'mon, Ashe, I guarantee you she'll be at Crystal at 11. I have a perfect solution for your worry. We're going to drop off Sana, and I'll take you somewhere that will ease your anxiety."

Sana watches him trying to cheer me up. "Danny, you have such a good heart to help your American friend."

"Thank you, *hayete*." Danny reaches over and kisses her hand.

"*Hayete*? Is that a nickname?" I ask, staring out the window at a part of Lebanon I've never seen before.

Winding down the road that leads from Mount Lebanon to the southern suburbs, the Hezbollah-ruled *banlieues* of the city, the residential buildings seem to be worn and empty. Most of the occupants are outside, staring at the cars passing by as they talk among themselves. Men with AK-47s slung over their shoulders pacing like jackals patrol their streets. All the women hide under waves of black burkas. This does not remind me of California at all.

"*Hayete* is like *habibi* but for a girl," Danny replies to my question that I've already forgotten I'd asked.

"Ashe, do not call any girl *hayete* unless you truly love her. If she is your life and you can't live without her. Right, Danny?" Sana elaborates as she looks intently at Danny, who's smiling.

"Okay, Ashe. We're almost there. You need to hide, get down." He throws me off as he pulls his baseball cap low on his forehead to hide his face.

Sana, like a cat, slinks into the backseat and quickly throws her Prada burka on. She's now unrecognizable, like a raindrop in the sea of black burkas outside.

"Make sure you look hot tonight, Sana. Everyone's going to be there," Danny says to her before she leaves.

"Okay, my love. I would never disappoint you." Tucked on the floor, I hear the door slam shut as she gets out of the car.

"Ashe, stay down. I'll let you know when you can get up."

I feel the car speeding up and making a few sharp turns and then come to a sudden stop. My heart sinks into the backseat floor mat as I hear Danny roll down the window to a shouting man's voice. Danny says something to him in Arabic and I hear the metallic clicking of a machine gun. It sounds like the conversation is escalating. I literally start reciting the *Our Father* in my head. Suddenly, I hear the window pull up and Danny starts slowly accelerating again.

"Sorry, *habibi*. I should've warned you. She lives in the heart of Hezbollah territory. The most dangerous part of Lebanon. They police themselves here. That's why we got stopped."

"Holy shit! An extremist Muslim terrorist group. Really? I don't think my heart can take this," I say from my fetal position on the car floor.

"We're good. We're in a BMW. They would never think we are here to blow it up. The suicide bombers never use the nice cars," Danny explains, still trying to reassure me in this insane situation.

"Whadda fuck is this? The Wild Wild East? How do I unsee what I just saw to continue to want to stay in Lebanon? Take me to the airport," I rant, still on the floor. "Danny, this is not what I signed up for. I want my ESPN fucking baseball games, popcorn and the fucking LAPD patrolling the streets."

"Okay, you can get up now," Danny chuckles as I sit up in the backseat.

"This isn't funny. I'm sure as hell they didn't buy those machine guns legally or have a permit," I yell at him, looking in the rearview mirror at his smiling face, unfazed by what just happened.

"Permits?" He laughs. "I told you. I'm gonna solve your security problems. You'll feel very safe in a few minutes. We're almost there."

We turn into some hilly side street and start driving up toward a bushy mountain. Danny makes a quick phone call, speaking in Arabic again. I don't know what's about to happen, but I know he has something planned.

He says we have to park on the shoulder of the road and walk. Up on the hill, I see a large concrete wall with a barbed-wire gate concealed with lush vegetation. The front door has a small call box on the wall.

Danny pushes the button as it beeps. "Marwan, we're here," he says into the call box. There's no response except for a buzzing sound of the moving camera above us.

After a few seconds, which feel like an eternity, the gate unlocks and we walk inside. The door shuts behind us automatically, and we find ourselves surrounded by shadows of untamed greenery. Suddenly, the three large panel doors in front of us, which were invisible till now, move counterclockwise, revealing the bright indoor area of a house no one would ever know was there.

The silent night is interrupted by the deafening sound of The Doors' "Riders on the Storm" as an illuminated figure appears walking toward us. It takes my eyes a minute to adjust to the amount of light behind him before I can see any details. With his arms outstretched, barefoot, with an enormous smile, his wild bird's-nest patch of long black hair tied in a loose man-bun, a long linen shirt and loose cotton pants, a ton of beads on his neck, wrists and ankles, he looks like a hippie from the future. The smell of burning Palo Santo engulfs the air, and I feel like I'm at Burning Man.

"Daaanyyyyy! My childhood best friend, welcome to my Nirvana!" he says in a spirited voice that goes together with the rest of him. Lean as a reed, with glittering green-grey eyes and a rugged, unshaven face, the guy seems likable enough, a legend of sorts, according to Danny.

"Marwan! You haven't changed one bit, brother," Danny says as they hug each other in a warm embrace.

"And you must be the Ashe he keeps telling me stories about." Marwan turns to me, smiling, before giving me an inviting hug. "Come... come inside. I just brewed some tea from Amsterdam for you."

"Thanks, it's nice to meet you. This is a bit of a surprise," I respond in awe of his energy.

We follow him through the corridors of this huge one-story house, filled with red curtains everywhere from ceiling to floor. It makes you feel you're in some Aladdin's cave of wonder. We walk on countless deep red and orange Persian rugs into a substantial living room and burning stone fireplace.

"Sit, please sit. Let's enjoy this wonderful hookah and tea." He puts aromatic coals in the hookah.

Inside his hidden hillside fortress, as the hookah smoke fills the air and the sugary peppermint tea warms me up, the light conversation eases me out of my anxiety.

"Mind if I use your bathroom?" I ask Marwan, feeling that the endless glasses of tea have gone straight to my bladder.

"Of course, Ashe. It's around the corner, straight ahead down the hallway," he replies mid-conversation with Danny, switching to Arabic as they continue their vibrant discussion.

I walk down the 50-foot hallway between the glass-tinted windows, from floor to ceiling, on one side and the lacquered, brown closet door panels on the other.

About ten feet away from the bathroom door, I notice the closet on my right is slid open. I'm not one to pry into people's business, but I just can't help but notice the lines of dozens of meticulously stacked RPG missile launchers in his closet. *Holy fucking shit!* The only time I've ever seen an RPG is in a Rambo movie. Suddenly I don't need to pee anymore. I turn around and speed-walk back to Danny, who is still sitting, laughing and having a good old time.

Standing next to Danny, I lean down and tap him on the shoulder, whispering, "We should really go."

"Relax, have a seat," he says between hookah puffs.

Marwan pulls out a gold AK-47, the Soviet-era assault rifle, from under his seat and fixes me with a wide-eyed, manic intensity. "Ashe, look. I wanted to show you this gem. Have you ever seen a beauty like this?"

"Oh my God, Marwan. That's insane. I want a picture with it," Danny says, laughing, as I stand there between the feeling of wanting to disappear and frozen with shock.

"Here you go, *habibi*. I got it for an African warlord. He's a good client of mine." He cheerfully admits to supplying mercenaries while handing Danny the machine gun.

Grinning widely, Danny poses with the gold AK-47 while Marwan snaps a couple of photos. "See, Ashe. I brought you to the best arms dealer in the whole Middle East."

"*Arms dealer?!* I saw your RPGs on the way to the bathroom and I freaked out. Danny doesn't tell me anything. Everything's a 'surprise,'" I say half-jokingly but terrified.

Marwan takes a deep toke of the hookah and puts his hand on my shoulder, amused. "You haven't seen anything yet, my friend. What you saw is just one percent of my shipments to Africa."

"Wow, you're not scared of the United States catching you?"

"I deal in the millions... the USA deals in the billions. I'm a bug on a windshield. They don't even notice me. The US is the war master of the world."

"Marwan, do you have anything small to make my friend feel more secure in Beirut?" Danny asks.

"Of course. I have many machine guns."

I shoot Danny a stone-cold glare.

"Which one would you like, Ashe?" Marwan asks kindly. "Or maybe you'd prefer a chrome Deagle?"

"I think I'm good... I'm good." I raise my hand in the air. "I need to digest all of this. But thank you, I appreciate your hospitality."

Danny looks at his watch, realizing it's getting late. "Well, Marwan. Always a pleasure to be in your presence." He gets up and they embrace goodbye. "Be safe, my friend. The night calls us."

Peeing on the side of the road outside Marwan's house, I breathe a sigh of relief to be out of that den.

"Whadda fuck?!" I say to Danny as we race back to the chalet to get ready for the nightclub.

"Just protecting you, brother."

"I'm happy we're still alive. All I could think of while at Marwan's was that a US drone would fly over us and bomb the shit out of his house. I could imagine the news saying, 'Three terrorists killed during an arms deal in Beirut' and no one would blink an eye."

Danny chuckles. "Just another Saturday in Beirut. That's why we always party as if it's the last night of our lives."

Just before 11 p.m., we arrive at Crystal, the city's most decadent club. Walking through the crowd of Lebanese beauties in short skirts and spiky heels outside the front door, I look for my blonde Cinderella among hundreds of dark heads. The doorman lets us in right away, and the VIP hostess walks us through the crowd to our table. Unexpectedly passing Amira and her large group partying, I avoid eye contact and march behind Danny.

Edging closer to our table, I see a blonde light in the darkness of this nightclub, which, like a wave, instantly washes away all my dusky thoughts. The relief in my heart that she is safe makes me feel like I'm floating toward her. She is standing with her back to me, wearing a slinky mauve dress that hugs her slight curves and shows off her toned and tanned legs. She is talking to Sana, and with her designer heels she is almost the same height. I rush past Danny and the hostess as Aleyna turns to me with a huge, sparkling smile. I sweep her up in an embrace and hold her like my life depends on it, without noticing that her feet are off the floor.

"Did you really miss me that much?" she says as Anwar, Michelle, Teddy and Sana greet Danny.

"I can't believe I found you."

"Is this for real?" she asks with a cute expression.

"You tell me. When I'm with you, nothing else matters. When I'm without you, I feel like I'm fading away," I say to her seriously. "I was so worried about you. You need to give me your phone number already."

"Worried? Why?"

"That guy who has been following me must've thought I was in your car. He drove after you when you left Johnny's resort. It was petrifying. I even went with Danny this afternoon to this wild arms dealer's house to get something to protect you," I continue to explain as the loud booming music engulfs us.

"Oh, Ashe. You're so cute, but I don't need to be protected by you. See, there's something I've been trying to tell you—"

I see from the corner of my eye, almost in a slow motion, Michelle bumping into Aleyna with her champagne glass and spilling it all over her beautiful mauve dress.

"Oh my God! I'm so sorry, Aleyna," Michelle says in a panic.

Before my girl can respond, Michelle quickly whisks her away. "Let's go to the bathroom real quick. I learned a trick while modeling in New York. I can fix this, honey. So sorry." She pulls Aleyna, grabs a bottle of sparkling Perrier and they disappear into the crowd.

Suddenly, I feel a hand on my shoulder. It's Chris from the US Embassy. A handsome white guy from Texas, in his 30s, Chris has become good friends with us over these past few months. He won't say exactly what he does, but it's obvious he has a high-ranking position. He waves to everyone at the table and then pulls me aside.

"Hey, Ashe, you look flustered. Everything okay?" he asks me with concern in his voice.

"Hey, brother. It's been an unbelievably crazy day. This armed guy has been following my girl and me, and I'm tripping out a bit. Trying to keep myself above the ground over here."

He just laughs. "I don't mean to burst your bubble, but many people in Beirut are armed, including in this club."

"Yeah, but they're not following me around Beirut."

"You're a good guy, so I'm going to tell you something I probably shouldn't. There was a file on you on the desk at the Embassy. I don't know the details, but if you're being followed,

I'd be *careful*," he says pointedly, and I feel the hair on my body stand up.

"A file on me? Why?" I say defensively. "I'm just a nobody."

"Listen, I'm going to give you a crash course on geopolitics in the Middle East. You see, you guys are bringing wealth to Lebanon, and the economic growth of this country is the last thing its neighbors want to see. Especially Israel. There's a lot of chatter in the background, and I think their eyes might zoom in on you."

"Wow. I must be the most naive American." Before I can utter another word, I notice Mephistopheles. "Holy shit, Chris! He's right there at the end of the bar."

"Who? Where? Don't look at him or point. Just describe him to me," he says, cool and calm, as he takes a sip of his drink.

"The guy I was telling you about. At the end of the bar, if you look over, to your right. Bald, well-built guy in the same blue suit from earlier today."

Chris stealthily finds a reflection of Mephistopheles in the bar mirror. "He looks like a trained asset. Maybe Mossad? I'd be cautious, but if you're with your girl, you should be safe."

"Whoa... wait a minute. What do you mean if I'm with my girl?"

"You don't know who Aleyna is?" Chris asks, perplexed.

"No. Who is she?"

"Oh, so she didn't tell you? Well, maybe she has her reasons. Damn, I've said way more than enough."

Michelle interrupts our conversation. "Hi, Chris, you cutie. Oh my gawd, this is my favorite song. Come dance with me!" She hangs on his arm, swaying her hips and pulling him to the dancefloor.

"Wait! Michelle, where's Aleyna?" I say, looking around and to my horror noticing that Mephistopheles is no longer at the bar.

"She said she needed to talk to someone and that she will be right back. What's wrong, babe? Have a drink. Loosen up," she says and vanishes with Chris into the crowded dancefloor.

I'm officially freaking out and stand up on our table, desperately trying to spot Aleyna's blonde hair among the darkness of heads in the crowd. I almost fall from the table as Danny yanks on my pants.

"*Habibi*," Danny says, smiling. "You're not going to believe this."

"Danny, please, not now. I have a huge problem."

"Dude, hear this one. First, Amira is fuming pissed. I just talked to her." He ignores what I just said and continues with the story. "Second, do you know what rich women hate the most?" he says and, without waiting for my reply, "Rich women with even more money!" He gestures a big circle with his arms.

"Why are you telling me this? This has nothing to do with me, and I'm in real fucking trouble here," I say, irritated, still anxiously scanning the club for Aleyna.

"*Habibi*, all your troubles are going to fade away when I tell you this. Ready? Aleyna is worth more than Amira. Her dad is a billionaire. He owns the Walmart of the Middle East. Only you, the motherfucking American Don Juan DeMarco, can come to Beirut and date not one but two billionaires in a matter of a few months," Danny says excitingly.

Turning around, I see her in her beautiful mauve dress and that incredible smile with her blonde hair illuminating her silhouette. I feel hugely relieved. Suddenly, like in a bad horror movie, I see Mephistopheles creeping up right behind her.

PARA TI HAYETE

"Out of all the choices, the honorable one is the most painful."

Standing motionless, I can't hear the music or Danny talking into my ear. My eyes are focused solely on Aleyna and Mephistopheles. Everyone in the club but her is dissolved, like in one of Salvador Dali's surrealist paintings. She walks straight up to me. My voice is imprisoned in my chest. I'm lost in her desert eyes.

"Ashe, I've been trying to tell you something important," she says, taking my hands into hers and pulling me close to ensure that I don't miss any of her words. "The man you thought was chasing us is actually my bodyguard. Let me introduce you to Tarek."

And just like that, Mephistopheles becomes Tarek. "Good to meet you, Mr. Ashe," he says with a gentle voice you wouldn't expect from someone who looks so menacing.

My body goes through the automatic motion of shaking his large hand, but I still can't hear my voice or feel my body in this dissociative trance.

Aleyna, seeing the consternation on my face, continues to talk to me. "I wanted to tell you earlier, but it was the first time someone saw me as I am and not as a monetary object. Being born into one of the wealthiest families in the Middle East, everyone here knows who I am, but you were different. My American, my dreamer who looks at me in a way that awakens every piece of my soul. I'm sorry for wanting to hold on to that unmarred feeling."

Sensing a private moment, Tarek interrupts, "Excuse me, Miss Aleyna, I'll be back by the bar if you need me."

Silently, she nods at him and looks back into my eyes as he walks away.

Napalm bombs of insight explode in my mind. My reality that existed just a few minutes ago has been decimated. From my tightened chest, only one word bubbles up to the surface, "Aleyna..."

"Yes, Ashe?" she says, squeezing my hands and allowing my voice to come back.

"I see you, all of you, and I get it. Hopefully that unmarred feeling will continue to follow all of our days together." I gently sweep her long blonde hair behind her ear and kiss her luscious lips.

The music roars, the crowd becomes noisy and I finally feel Danny's patting on my back.

"*Habibi*, I don't wanna leave without you. We're going to continue the party in our chalet. The vibe in this club is done."

"Really, we just got here?"

"Oh bro, your sense of time is way off today. You have been in la-la land holding this girl's hands for the past hour," he says, laughing.

"Oh, shit." I realize he's right.

"Is something wrong?" Aleyna asks as Danny, Sana and Michelle start slowly heading toward the door.

"How can anything be wrong with you around? We're just leaving the club." Holding her hand, I guide her toward the exit as I glimpse at Tarek following us at a distance and at Amira's vacant table.

The parking outside of the club is filled with Dayglo-colored Lamborghinis and Ferraris. I have never seen this many exotic supercars revving in one place.

Aleyna pulls on my hand a few feet away from Danny's car. "Ashe," she says in a wistful tone.

"Yes?" I reply, sensing something is wrong. "We're heading back to party at our chalet. Did you not want to come?"

"I'd love to go with you, but I can't tonight."

"I'm confused. You want to go but you can't?"

"Oh, my sweet American, it would bring a great dishonor to me and my family to be seen leaving this place with a man at this time of night."

"Wow! I keep forgetting that I'm not in LA and you keep reminding me you're unlike anyone I've ever met before." Still,

I can't help wondering if she's being a little coy. "Will I see you again?"

"If it's meant to be, you will," she replies with a deep stare and puts her hand on my face. With her other hand, she slips into mine a small object and smiles before walking away to her car.

Danny, honking and hanging out his car window, is shouting at me to hurry. I look at my hand to discover a small matchbox from Crystal. Aleyna gets into her car, looks back at me one more time, and winks. I shake the box, realizing its empty. I slide it open with excitement. Inside, in a neat handwriting, is a phone number with a heart. I find it incredibly endearing. When I look up to express my happiness, her car is gone.

The next morning, Abdul's prayer is a welcoming reminder that the sun is coming up soon and I'm blessed with another day here. While rolling back his prayer rug, he looks up at me curiously. "You're usually asleep at this time. I hope I didn't wake you."

"Not at all, brother. I like your song prayers. They're so calming. This morning, my emotions won't allow me to sleep any longer, as I bask in the memories of her, longing to see her again. There's a rule I live by, not to call a girl the next day after you get her number because it makes you look desperate."

"Oh, Aleyna finally gave you her number."

"It's a gift and a curse at the same time. It's tearing me up inside because I really want to call her. Now," I vent to Abdul.

"It's 5:36 A.M., I don't know... maybe wait a couple hours?" he says proudly, feeling like he is giving me sound advice. I laugh inside and eventually end up calling her at 7:19 A.M.

"Hi, it's Ashe," I say warily, not knowing what to expect.

"Hey, it's Aleyna." She sounds very much awake and I sense a smile in her voice.

"Did I wake you?" I ask like a dumbass.

"Oh, no. I've been up since 5:30 A.M. I do my yoga and go for a run in the morning."

"Wish I would've known that a couple of hours ago. Maybe I would've joined you," I say, laughing, realizing I just spent the past two hours looking pointlessly at the clock on the wall.

"Well, if you're still interested in seeing me today, you can accompany me for a few errands I have to tend to."

"I'd love to."

"It won't be anything glamorous like you're used to."

"Any time with you is perfect. I'm ready," I say swiftly.

"Wonderful. I'll pick you up in 15 minutes." Without giving me a chance to say "bye," she hangs up.

I shower, dress and I'm ready in less than 10 minutes. As I'm walking out of the bathroom, Danny is grinning at the table, enjoying his morning coffee and fig rolls, replying to emails.

"Dude, how many Ashe beautification steps did you just skip? I have never seen you get ready this fast."

"Aleyna is picking me up any minute to go someplace I don't know."

"Wow! You're ready and on time? She's already changing you for the better." Danny smiles as we hear a gentle honk outside.

Walking up to her car and seeing her beautiful face fills me with such joy. I notice her car is filled to the brim with books and school supplies. The only empty space is my seat.

"Good morning... I'm so happy to see you. Are you starting a library?"

"Get in! You'll see. We have many stops to make," she replies, smiling as I fasten my seatbelt and notice in the side mirror that Tarek is driving behind us.

Our first stop is a small elementary school on the outskirts of Beirut. The building is an old, one-story shanty structure with broken windows. She gets out of her BMW and immediately a swarm of kids shouting her name surrounds her. She motions for me to unload the school goodies from her car. After the many thanks by the teacher and countless hugs from the kids, we're off to the next stop.

I'm completely in awe. "Aleyna, I'm speechless and it touches me deeply seeing the happiness in those kids' eyes. This is such an incredible act of kindness from you."

"They are the future of my country, it's the least I can do. Education is power."

"Those books were like a long-awaited Christmas gift for them. I've never seen kids be so grateful and hungry for knowledge. Something that, as an American, I've always taken for granted. It's really humbling to see." I look out the window, reminiscing about my childhood against the backdrop of the Lebanese mountains.

"I'm glad you feel that way. We have three more stops this morning. The need is so great. This is just a drop in the sea," she replies as she turns up her house music and intertwines her right hand into mine.

After the last stop, I realize, thanks to her, I now know a different Lebanon and a different Aleyna. What a stark contrast she is to the other rich people I've met in my life. Interestingly, she couldn't care less about what you have or what you drive. What she seems to value the most is a spiritual wealth and knowledge.

Our conversations for the next weeks involve our purpose in the world, the change we would like to see, love, politics and lots of laughter, which only cements our relationship. It feels like we have known each other our whole lives. Sometimes you don't realize you're falling hard in love with someone until you've already fallen.

Living in the moment in Beirut feels like the nights are orchestrated by angels. Our romantic candlelit dinners are followed by incredible nights out dancing, truly living as if it's our last night on earth. Just like Danny said, "the Beirut way."

The success of Danny's beach-resort parties grows into a frantic pace leading up to the 50 Cent concert, which is coming up in less than two weeks. Everyone wants a piece of us now. Danny has multiple investors begging for a way in with us. A far cry from where he started, unsure if this would even materialize the way he envisioned. We're literally changing the music scene in Lebanon and the rest of the world is taking notice.

"Judge Jules in Beirut! We did it, boys! 50 Cent is next, then Erick Morillo!" Danny raises his champagne glass next to Sana, surrounded by old and new friends in one of the most luxurious beach resorts in Lebanon.

Glancing around, I see Michelle with her new Italian boy-friend alongside Anwar and Abdul toasting Danny with smiles on their faces. The guest list is full, but there are still crowds of people outside dying to come in to experience a well-known DJ from England.

Danny pulls me aside. "I need to ask you a huge favor."

"Yes, of course, brother."

"Yo, *habibi*, I've never seen my boy so happy. What is it? Does this girl have some golden pussy or what?" he says, chuckling into my ear.

"Well, I wouldn't know." I blush, being caught off guard.

"Are you serious? You haven't closed the deal yet? I never would have guessed. The chemistry between you two is like fire."

"Aleyna is an incredible woman, and our relationship is much deeper than physical," I say honestly.

"Dude, she's really changing you. I've never seen you like this, bro."

"I've never seen you light up so much as you do around Sana."

"It's happening. I have contracts, *habibi*. Jay-Z, Shakira in Beirut and Dubai, our dreams are coming true and look at us, fools in love in Lebanon. I feel like we're going to stay for good," Danny says prophetically.

"When I look at Aleyna, I see it too. For the first time I don't miss the Cali sunsets, I look forward to the Beirut sunrises."

"You're the only person I trust here. It pains me to ask this of you right now. But I need you to go to Egypt with one of my big ballers arriving in from LA. Just for three days, flying out tomorrow. He wants in on my projects. I need a VIP host, someone to entertain him, smooth him over. I was going to go but I have to stay and tidy up shit around the venue for 50 Cent."

"Is that all? I got you, *habibi*. Don't worry. I'll make sure he has a fantastic time and comes back in one piece." I give him a hug.

"I can always count on you. That's why you're my best friend. Seems like I've taken you away from Aleyna for too long." He winks and taps me on the shoulder, noticing Aleyna walking toward us. She is wearing a black halter-neck dress with a simple gold pendant. Her long blonde hair falls in waves around her beautiful face.

"It's a lovely party, Danny. Congratulations!" she says as she takes my hand. "But can I borrow your best friend for a minute?"

"Of course, my dear. I have to go find Sana." He waves as he walks away.

I look at Aleyna, mesmerized by her bronze eyes. "You look so incredibly alluring against this sunset."

"It's a perfect time for a walk on the beach, come." Her teeth sparkle against the French red lipstick.

As we walk down by the seashore, I notice Tarek behind us.

"Do you ever feel weird knowing someone is always following you?" I ask as she turns around to look at Tarek.

"I'm used to it and it gives my father a peace of mind since I was a victim of many kidnapping attempts when I was a little girl. I really don't want to talk about it because I have something uplifting to say."

"I apologize. I'm just a regular guy who's ignorant of such things." Sensing her unease, I change the subject. "What would you like to share?"

"Well, our one-month anniversary is tomorrow, and I was thinking..." She starts as she pulls me closer. The warm waves of the Mediterranean crash at our feet. Looking up at me lovingly, she says, "There's a cozy boutique hotel tucked away in the mountains near a waterfall. I booked us a room for a couple of nights to celebrate us. Is that okay?" Gazing for a confirmation in my eyes, she squeezes my hands.

"*Hayete*," I say softly.

"*Hayete?* Really?" She smiles and kisses me passionately on the lips, giving me a little taste of what the getaway entails.

This can't be happening. Not now.

"This is painful, but I don't know how to sugarcoat it, so I'll just be honest with you, angel. There's nothing I want more than to spend some time alone with you under a hidden waterfall, lost in your eyes... lost in Beirut," I say, weaving my fingertips through her long blonde waves as I rest my forehead on hers.

"But?" she asks in a soft, dispirited tone.

"I literally just gave my word to Danny that I will accompany his business partner to Egypt for three days. It means so much to him. He has no one else who can do it. We're leaving tomorrow morning. Is there a way you can reschedule this incredible adventure for when I get back?" I say, seeing the disappointment in her eyes.

"Wow, even after so many months in Beirut, you're still stuck in your American ways. When will you learn that tomorrow is promised to no one? Live your life like others can only imagine or all the magic will pass you by," she says sulkily as her body stiffens.

I stand in silence, unable to find the right words, so I kiss her forehead.

"We are free to make our own choices, Ashe, and like I said before, what's meant to be will be," Aleyna says unapologetically.

As the sun is setting behind us, she lets go of my embrace and walks away. Her footprints in the sand disappear with the crashing waves.

A BLIND MAN'S PAPYRUS

"Does the ancient stone remember the hand that shaped it?"

The 90-minute flight from Beirut to Cairo teaches me how to cry without weeping and is too short to enjoy first class. As it turns out, Danny's big baller is a well-known club owner and real-estate developer from Los Angeles named Sonny. His company, full of charm and wit, is a much-needed distraction from the ache I feel missing Aleyna. If laughter is a remedy for sadness, Sonny has got the cure. His excitement to explore Egypt is infectious.

Getting off the plane, two young men approach us to carry our luggage. These two baggage carriers were smart to pick Sonny out of all the passengers arriving on our flight. He reeks of status. His large build, slicked-back black hair, goatee, tattoos and expensive designer clothes make him look like a caricature out of an Italian gangster movie. Only that Sonny is Assyrian. A Middle Eastern version of Robert De Niro. The no-nonsense, take-shit-from-nobody attitude is a refreshing reminder of home. We hit it off instantly, just as Danny had predicted.

Nearing the airport exit, we come to an abrupt stop. Our baggage handlers have put down our luggage and are kneeling on the floor together, which infuriates Sonny.

"Why the fuck did you just put my luggage on the floor? Get the fuck up or I'm not tipping you. I want to get to our hotel," he commands them.

He takes their silence as an indicator they don't understand English, but when they start to bow in prayer, I put my hand on his shoulder to signal "ease off on them."

And, suddenly, over the clamor of the airport, the call to prayer drifts out softly from a nearby mosque into the blazing afternoon heat. As his anger simmers, I turn around and it hits me. My eyes cannot believe it. I tap him to lower himself as I get on my knees.

"The fuck you doin' down there too, Ashe? Is everyone going mad in Cairo?" he says, in refusal to lower himself.

Without a word, I point to the whole airport behind us. Sonny's mouth drops. Realizing that he's the only one standing, he squats down grudgingly. We are not in LA anymore. Everyone at this airport is on their knees for the Dhuhr salat, a Muslim noon prayer. All business and locomotion have ceased. In all my time in the Middle East, I have never seen a sight like this. It frightens me because, again, I'm a minority. Here, religion clearly comes before business, before everything. Frustrated, Sonny throws some money at the two baggage carriers, who are still praying with their eyes closed. He then picks up the bags himself and starts heading toward the exit. I follow him outside the airport only to see Egypt on pause there as well. No car is moving. The cab drivers are out of their cars, on their knees, in prayer.

"For fuck's sake, you gotta be kidding me!" Sonny drops the bags and starts laughing. We break out in a chuckle just in time for Egypt to unfreeze again. It takes only seconds before a cab driver comes running to offer his services to us. Sonny won't agree to hire him until he sees what this man is driving. Happy with the make of the car, we're finally on our way to the hotel.

If there are divider lanes on these streets of Cairo, no one can find them, especially our driver. The tiny cars squeeze inches from each other in all sorts of directions. Cars and pedestrians all whisked together in complete chaos, which somehow works.

Our hotel on the Nile River is picturesque. A beautiful mixture of contemporary architecture and old corbel vaulted ceilings. Larger than what I thought it would be. The first thing I do when we get to our penthouse suite is call Aleyna. Her phone just rings as I sit there with my head down until Sonny tells me to hang up.

"Let's go grab dinner on the Nile," he says cheeringly. The thought of dinner on the longest river in the world is better than my impulse of calling her again.

Just before the sun begins to set, we head out to the fancy restaurant on the Nile. It isn't quite what we expected. It's a river boat docked on the actual Nile River. The food is excellent, and the view is breathtaking. At the adjacent table, we meet a lovely photographer from New York City and her family. Born and raised in Cairo, she offers us some priceless advice to travel to Sharm el-Sheikh, a small city on the Red Sea. Her gentleness, gorgeous smile and thoughtful tourism suggestion prompts Sonny to pay hundreds of dollars for her and her family's dinner. That's Sonny's style, to show appreciation when it's due.

As the sun rises higher on the horizon in the morning, the pyramid complex is more majestic than our minds can comprehend. Khufu, Khafre and Menkaure are no longer trapped in my small television or on a textbook page. They are free, gloriously rising above the burnt-orange desert sands all the way to their Egyptian deities. The Sahara, stretching for millions of scorched square miles against the deepest blue sky, is a little surreal and soul-stirring. After the predictable party madness and crowd-heaving nightclubs of Beirut, the emptiness of the desert is incredibly soothing.

Sonny asks me to slow down as he takes more and more pictures, but my pounding heart propels me forward, almost against my will.

The red-hot sun beats down its 120-degree heat. Staring at the light reflected off the dunes, mesmerized, I hear Rodger Henderson's spirited voice carried on the balmy sirocco winds of the Sahara, *"Fill the vessel... fill the vessel..."* I fall to my knees in tears on a large ancient rock and open myself to the wonder before me. The nomad has awakened.

Sonny stares at me, stunned, shaking his head. "Wow, Danny mentioned you were different. Little out there and I didn't believe him. But, brother, I've never met anyone like you. Everyone's looking at you right now."

"Sharm el-Sheikh is calling our names, brother," I grin, wiping tears from my cheeks as I rise off the rock.

"You're one crazy motherfucker. I love it," he replies, smiling. "You know what's the best part about having fuck-you money? You can do whatever the fuck you want. Let's go."

As we head out of the complex with a buzz of excitement in our hearts and big smiles on our faces, I notice a small, charming, busy art gallery. The walls are covered in all sorts of the most gorgeous papyrus art I have ever seen in my life. Not the cheap printouts you can find at the airport shops, but the true museum-quality art pieces.

An elderly man stands out from the crowd, sitting elevated in the middle of the gallery. His cane and dark glasses are an enigma to me, so I inquire about him with one salesperson. Turns out the blind man is the artist behind these works of art. The salesperson tells me the artist went blind recreating and using the highly toxic metallic paints used by the Egyptians thousands of years ago.

The blind old man, overhearing our conversation, says to me, "Things we create change us."

I learn that these metallic papyrus paintings are one-of-a-kind and when they're gone, no one else will dare to make them this way again. *Sold!* Thinking of Aleyna, I subconsciously gravitate to the papyrus representing a pharaoh's wedding. Sonny buys three other pieces of art for himself and we're off again.

Waking up in Sharm el-Sheikh is much different than waking up in Cairo. The relaxed Red Sea beach resort town, tucked between the sea and desert on the southernmost tip of the Sinai Peninsula, is a breath of fresh air away from the bustling, excruciatingly overcrowded city. I never dreamed I would see such a beautiful contrast. The Egyptian desert bleeding into the crystal blue Red Sea. We spend the mornings scuba diving and the afternoons quad biking in the desert. At night, we explore all the wonderful restaurants and hookah bars.

On our last night we end up at Pacha, the best nightclub in town. In a beautiful crowd, Sonny draws the attention of three gorgeous blonde Russian female tourists. They sit at our table and party with Sonny all night. Their company makes me miss Aleyna even more. Resisting their charms, I whisper to Sonny that I will meet him back at the hotel later.

"Ashe, you're such a weirdo. She has answered none of your calls. These girls here are all over us," Sonny replies in my ear and reaches to pour me some more Dom Perignon. "It's our last night. Have some fun."

I put my hand on his shoulder, smile and walk out of the club as he smiles back.

Getting back to the hotel, I walk straight past the blue mosaic fountain, past our room and straw cabana umbrellas, which are illuminated by the coming dawn. I walk without hesitation along the palm-fringed promenade to the sea's edge. The coral gardens of the Red Sea are calling, inviting me to the sunrise party for one. I have a vision of Aleyna's reflection in the glassy green waters.

Clenching a Motorola cellphone in my hand, I sit down on the rough coral shore. As the sun peaks its head through the shimmering azure sea, I dial Aleyna's number. It rings three times and then, "Hello?"

MIDSUMMER NIGHT'S BALLAD

"Waterfalls echo in my dreams."

My skin is still lathered with the rich, healing mineral salts of the Red Sea as we land back in Beirut. Some journeys heal deep wounds and remind you to allow in the new, despite all the fear you carried for years in your heart. As our plane lands, Sonny's story of the escapade with the Russians last night has me in a cheerful mood. Smiling, we walk through the terminal and, unexpectedly, there she is, standing in front of her car, in a flowing white summer dress, blonde hair tangled by the wind, as if she's swimming in the air. I can't believe she showed up at the airport for me. That unpredictability makes her even more thrilling to be with, that and her gentle nature and sweetness.

Sonny gives me a hug and says with a smile that he'll see me later, running off to the taxi. The next steps I take toward Aleyna happen in slow motion. The thrill in my chest reaches a detectable decibel level and then she smiles.

"Do you know what's the best part about coming back from a trip?" she asks, looking into my eyes as I stand, unsure of the circumstances.

"Seeing you?" I say, putting down my luggage to free my hands.

"That you're already packed to come with me," Aleyna says as I inch closer, wondering if I have permission to embrace her.

She turns around as her long blonde hair blows inches away from my face, purposefully, so she can taunt me with her gorgeous scent, and gets into the driver's seat.

She pokes her head out. "Are you getting in?"

Standing there, glassy-eyed, I take a few seconds to realize what's happening. In this waking dream, the nomad cannot hesitate and so I jump into the car.

Leaving the airport, passing Beirut, passing Jounieh and rising into the mountains, we listen to her house music, a perfect soundtrack for the landscapes surrounding us. Other than a couple of glances at each other, we drive without words, content with each other's company. It's at this moment I realize I haven't seen Tarek or his car following us, but I don't want or care to bring it up. For it's the first time I feel like we're alone and it's liberating. My smile grows with every mile we drive farther into the lost mountains.

A couple hours pass until she speaks. "Can you hear it?" She looks at me and puts the window down. As we rumble slowly along dusty crooked roads, I see a glistening waterfall peek its tail out. The loud comforting sound of the billion water drops crashing on the ancient mountain lifts my breath to exhale. This delightful moment culminates with her hand gripping mine. The first touch since I left for Egypt sends shivers down my spine. I never noticed it before, but Aleyna, just like me, has a tiny scar between the index and middle finger of her right hand. When we hold hands, I see her scar become one with mine, like the river running into the sea.

I bring it to her attention and she smiles. "Some lovers get matching tattoos. We have matching scars. Every time I look at my hand now, I'll think of you. We're here."

Our hotel, perched on a cliff, has a small facade that leads into a long, large complex. The suite she chose for us is located high on the mountain, hanging over the lush valley and magnificent waterfall from a ginormous balcony.

Watching this primordial wonder, huge shafts of icy water dropping through a limestone cave, feels exhilarating. I lean over the rails of our room's balcony, mesmerized.

"Aren't you afraid of falling, Ashe?"

"Aleyna, can't you see? I've already fallen."

"Saying less is always best," she says, slowly approaching me with a dreamy look in her eyes. "Show me."

With the beat of the waterfall and heat of the red sunset, I lift her up. My head lost in her flowing blonde hair, her legs gently wrap around my waist, and our lips collide. We become one. The air she exhales fills my lungs and intensifies the fire inside me. Her naked beauty magnifies and shimmers in our candlelit room till early morning.

Our six-course meal is brought to the room the next morning since she doesn't want anyone to see her in town. This is her time, this is our life, this is our private love. Playing backgammon on the balcony in our robes, eating grapes and enjoying the local red wine, time disappears.

Mischievously, she mentions she has a gift for me. After rifling through her bag, she returns with two small portable speakers and a tiny ornate box. Aleyna sets up the speakers and starts a music playlist. The music is quite original: house mixed with a Middle Eastern twist.

"This is for you." She hands me the tiny gold box. Inside are two white pills with a seated Buddha engraved on them.

I laugh and say, "Buddhas, huh? The best... seems I can't escape LA."

"They were hard to get in Lebanon. I've been waiting for someone special to experience them with." She turns up the music and pours us a glass of red wine.

Swallowing the little white pills, we look into each other's eyes like a pair of kids going up a new ride at Disneyland. The beat of the music pulsates in our veins and electrifies our souls as we laugh, touch, dance, burning throughout the moonlit evening.

The ceiling-to-floor white curtains sway with the wind, in and out of the balcony's open French doors. She is naked, embraced in my arms as her teary eyes bring my body to a pause.

She leans in, my face wrapped in her hair, and then she places her scarred hand on my chest and whispers, "I buried my feelings for you, for a night just like this. In Lebanon we only have now. I love you, Ashe."

"This must be the ecstasy talking," I reply with a grin but pull her closer. "Aleyna, since the moment I saw you at Bread and Brown, my heart has been yours."

"Would you still love me if I had nothing?" she asks out of an impulse.

"If I have just you, I have everything."

She kisses me before I can say another word. My hands lay her back onto the bed as she opens her legs and I kiss her tanned, muscular stomach and continue lower. "It is ecstasy, my love, but not the pill, it's you and your wicked tongue, so gently licking honey off my butterfly's wings." She gasps. "I touch the sky when you're in my arms."

We burn like Jupiter's orange clouds, moving tirelessly in its hurricane in our cedar mountain hideaway.

Three days pass, carved with euphoria into our episodic memory. We don't look at each other the same way anymore, holding hands through the entire drive back to Jounieh. With her, I feel I found something great, possibly lasting, and suddenly it's hard to imagine going back home to California. Parked in front of Danny's chalet, crouched in our car seats, gazing at each other, we resist splitting. As I trace the scar on her hand with my finger, the door is thrown wide open. Two big men grab me by the shirt and neck and forcefully drag me out of her car.

Aleyna screams at them in Arabic. Ten feet away, I am shoved into the backseat of a dark suv. Blindfolded, with a black sack over my head, I feel the driver speeding up as I hear Aleyna's shouting voice fade away.

LOVE IS BLINDNESS

"Once in a while, our paths lead us to an unforeseen tollway."

The speeding black SUV screeches to an abrupt stop and I'm flung onto the seat in front of me. All these months in Beirut and I still can't understand the language. I can't understand a single word these men are shouting.

"*Yallah*, get out!" a man yells at me as I hear the door fling open.

I'm frozen and can't feel my legs. Just like a child at the doctor's closing my eyes before a shot, I don't want them to take the black bag off my head. Somehow, the darkness is comforting. I was just getting to know this wonderful girl and now I'm being kidnapped and possibly killed. If these are my last minutes as an American in the Middle East, I'm hoping to get the lead and not the knife. Imagining my mom and dad opening a box mailed to them with my finger or ear sent for ransom makes me nauseous and dizzy. I can barely breathe.

"*Yallah, yallah*! Get out, Ashe," the man yells again and his voice sounds strangely familiar.

Someone rips the black sack off my head. My eyes squint from the bright Lebanese sun. As my pupils focus on the face in front of me, I can't believe what I see.

It's Tarek, surrounded by five armed men in army fatigues, with a grave look on his face. He escorts me out of the car in front of this dazzling-white palace high on a hill. Coming from LA, I've partied in some of the mega mansions in Bel-Air, and this estate dwarfs them all. It's so big and sprawling it intimidates me. Tarek pushes me forward, leading us up the white marble steps into a large, open foyer. I see the abundant staff quickly part away deeper into the complex, closing doors behind them. Taking the imperial stairway up to the second floor, my heart is beating wildly in my chest.

"Tarek, can I ask you something?" I say, panting, walking slowly while I hold on to an ornamented railing. The aggressive shove he gives me is my answer.

Down the long hall is a sizable library with a fireplace and a balcony overlooking the hill. Tarek guides me in. Outside on the balcony, an older gray-haired man with an icy gaze is sitting at a small coffee table, watching me enter the room while he enjoys his tea. Completely unfazed by the terror on my face or what I went through to get here, he slurps loudly. He points at the chair in front of him, his wrist accessorized with a gold Patek Philippe watch.

"Sit!" Tarek commands and then leaves me alone with the old man.

Hot and flushed from having a sack over my head, I slump down into the armchair. I immediately notice a large orange manila envelope on the coffee table in front of him. He sits reclined, with one leg over his knee, sipping his black tea, leering at me. His tanned, clean-shaven, wrinkled face is almost expressionless, except that his eyes cannot hide his hatred toward me.

I did nothing to this old man. I've never seen him before in my life. *Did Danny cross the wrong person, putting up the largest concert ever in Lebanon? Am I being held ransom for something? Was that the last time I'll ever see Aleyna? And how the fuck is Tarek involved in all of this?*

While I sit and stare back, unflinching, into the old man's cold eyes, I keep replaying in my mind getting abducted in broad daylight. I'm so rattled by the intrusion that I can't stand the silence and suspense any longer and blurt out, "Who are you?"

"The more important question to ask, Ashe, is why are you here?" he replies dryly in perfect English.

"You're right. Why am I here? And who are you to kidnap me in the middle of the day, snatching me away from the love of my life?" I shoot back, no longer hiding how pissed off I am.

He sets his teacup down and leans toward me. "You mean Aleyna, my daughter?" he says slowly but with a raised voice. "The love of my life you dared to snatch away from me and my protection?!"

Oh shit!

This is slowly making sense as the curtain is being pulled back and I see the bigger picture. Ditching Tarek, never leaving our hotel room and turning off her phone, Aleyna's cleverness makes me admire her even more. I look around, scanning my surroundings for her, as I realize I'm sitting in her family home.

"She's not here. This is between you and me, and it's going to stay that way."

I nod my head in acceptance of his terms. He forcefully slides the manila envelope to my side of the coffee table.

"Do you know why my daughter requires protection?" he says, looking over the balcony as if the past is there.

"Yes, she has mentioned that to me briefly," I reply, seeing the pain in his eyes.

He sits there for several slow, torturous minutes, resting his chin on his hand, as though deep in thought.

"I know who you are, Ashe. You think I would allow you to be around my daughter without knowing absolutely everything about you?" he says, pointing to the envelope. "Look, it's all there. No arrests, privately schooled in Notre Dame and CalArts, even changed your name because your biological father never cared to raise you."

I open the envelope and the first thing that screams off the page is my full name. I see my whole life documented in front of me. It's a surreal feeling. This must be the file at the US Embassy that Chris was trying to tell me about.

I lean toward him. "Everything in here is correct. I have nothing to hide, but I have something to say to you. Your daughter is the most marvelous human I've ever had the privilege to know. She fills my days with wonder and gives me hope for a better future. My heart is rekindled knowing a woman like her even exists—"

"*Future?*" He stops me in shock.

"Yes, sir. Emphatically," I reply, unruffled.

"Let me tell you about the future, Ashe, so we are both on the same page." He stands up, putting his hands on the balcony railing, a king overlooking his empire. "Come here," he commands. "Let me show you."

Just wanting this to be over with, I stand up and warily join him on the balcony.

"Over there is the house of my daughter Clara." He points to a large roof peeking out of a stand of towering cedars on the right side of the hill. The palatial house, with its swimming pool, rolling lawns and citrus trees, could easily be mistaken for some cushy palace in Bel-Air or Beverly Hills.

"And over there will be the house of Aleyna when she's married," he says as his hand encircles the other side of the hill.

"Aleyna's house?" I ask, flustered.

"In your culture, you have nothing unless you have money. In my culture, you have nothing unless you have a family. My family stays with me. This is the only way I can protect them from my enemies. Here, Ashe." He points to the estate and adds fiercely, "Not in America, not in LA, but here. In Beirut. She stays here. You understand me?"

It is at this moment I come face to face with a life-changing decision. I never imagined that love's price would be so high.

I nod silently, feeling the weight of his terms.

He grips the balcony railing harder. "Aleyna is my youngest, and she has a gentle, loyal soul," he says, looking out into the distance. "With her, your life will be changed forever. Money will no longer be an issue for you, but eventually the diamonds will not sparkle, and the fancy cars will just rust. Your current hustle for money will be replaced by fear. The ever-growing fear for your loved one's safety because as the houses get bigger, the walls become taller. The paradise everyone sees from afar is nothing but a gilded prison. Wealth buys you few friends and lots of enemies. When you are as old as I am, you can tell a good man when you see one. I see you are a good man, Ashe, but do you have the strength to love my daughter?"

Standing stoic, with a controlled, slow breath, the only sign of distress I feel inside from the weight of his words is the virtuous floater storm that occupies my sight. I look deep into his peering eyes and say, "I love your daughter and I would die for her."

He gets closer to my face and with an accepting tone replies, "Well, my son, in Lebanon, you just might." He taps me on the shoulder and strolls away.

I stand there in disbelief before I get escorted out by Tarek and sent back to Jounieh.

When I get dropped off back home, Danny opens the door to the chalet before I can turn my key. With a relieved look on his face, he pulls me inside and hugs me tight.

"Man, what happened to you?" he asks, "Aleyna was here like 20 minutes ago, looking for you. Are you okay?"

Anwar, Abdul and Michelle rush over to hug me. I slump down into the couch, a little shaken but surrounded by my friends.

"I'm not okay. I'm fucking far from okay. I'm actually exactly the opposite of okay."

"Oh my God, Ashe. What happened? I was so worried. You, like... vanished." Michelle flaps her hands in a squiggly gesture. Abdul and Anwar just sit there, intently waiting for me to spill the tea.

"Well, Aleyna's father wanted to have a chat with me so he sent me an invitation I could not refuse," I say sarcastically.

"Wow, that's awesome, Ashe. You met her dad. That's good. That's a good thing, right?" Michelle says, cheerfully puzzled by the lack of excitement on my face just as the doorbell rings. Without waiting for my reply, she adds, "Oh, that's my date. Well, I'm glad you're okay, honey. Catch up later." She gives me a hug and kiss on the cheek and rushes out the door to her Italian boyfriend.

"*Habibi*, I guess that makes two of us then. I met Sana's father last night," he says, his eyes widening.

"This is new," I say, sensing my best buddy wants to vent.

"I drove to Dahieh to meet him."

"No?!" Abdul looks shocked. "That's the heart of Hezbollah, the Shi'ite Islamist stronghold. She lives there?"

"Ha! Hold your breath, it gets better." Danny pauses as Anwar watches us speechless, munching loudly on his almonds, like a kid in a movie theater "There I was, huddled in a small living room with her father. The bitter tea and dry conversation turned serious when I found out he's actually a Hezbollah militant, but that wasn't the worst part."

Anwar nearly chokes on his almonds while Abdul and I unanimously shout, "NOOO!"

"Listen to this crazy shit, boys," Danny continues with a chuckle. "He puts his two fingers together, right to my face, and mentions a dowry. One hundred thousand dollars for his daughter's hand."

"So what did you tell him?" I ask, amazed.

"Sure, and that I'm going to call my CPA in the morning."

All of us fall about laughing.

"CPA? Which one of us is your CPA?" Anwar asks, rising from the sofa. "Okay, brothers. We're glad you're both still alive, let's try to keep it that way. Abdul, let's go. We're going to be late for the meeting. A lot to do before this concert tomorrow."

Abdul gets up and they rush out the door to meet one of Danny's clients.

After the laughter fades from the room with Abdul and Anwar leaving, I sit there with Danny in an eerie silence till he finally comes out with, "Ashe, I'm ten years older than you and I can tell you that one day, you will be an old man, looking back at your life, and this moment will haunt you. Not because of the chances you took but because of what you've walked away from."

I stare at him wistfully. The truth brings tears to my eyes.

"What are the chances of you becoming a great artist, actor or whatever? No one knows, but you know what life has given you at this moment," he says with a wisdom in a soft voice that is a rare occurrence to hear from Danny. "Haven't you learned in Lebanon yet that the present is the only thing that matters?"

"Danny, I have nothing to offer her. I still have achieved nothing I'm proud of. I'm still not a man—"

"*Habibi*," he cuts me off, "you're the best man I know and she's a billionaire. There's absolutely nothing materialistic in this world she could want from you. Love is not an exchange, it's a gift. Stay here."

I look into his eyes and then out the window toward the sea of ancient cedar groves. "That's just it, Danny. If I stay in Lebanon, I can never go back home. That's the price of our love."

FATA MORGANA

"The beating drums no one could hear but the world would see."

Rushing against the clock, I pick up my order, for the only licensed 50 Cent concert T-shirts, from a local clothing factory. It's a simple white T-shirt with 50 Cent's face splashed across it, beneath "Live in Beirut" and Danny's logo. I can barely fit a thousand meticulously wrapped and folded memorabilia into Danny's BMW. The concert is starting in three hours and there's still more staff I need to hire to help me sell all of this merchandise. Luckily, Danny's younger brother has seven friends who would love to make money tonight. There's an electricity in the air throughout the entire city in anticipation of this event. The largest ever sold-out concert in Lebanon has been the only topic in town for days.

Preoccupied, I haven't been able to see Aleyna since my ordeal with her father. Once she learned I was all right, we agreed, over the phone, to meet for the after-party at the SkyBar on the waterfront. Even though I offered many times for her to join me in the VIP area, she declined. She doesn't care for hip hop. My eyes and heart long for her, but the quick pace of this night distracts me.

With dozens of Lebanese army soldiers guarding the BIEL, it's the safest I have felt since I've been in Beirut. It reminds me of all the security I would see going to concerts at the Hollywood Bowl.

The concertgoers' cars trickle in, one by one, like ants weaving their way into the parking lot. Bumper to bumper, this allows my sales team to sell out all my T-shirts, except for the 33 that I keep for family and friends.

As a reward, I walk my sales team into the concert free of charge, straight to the VIP area next to the stage. In LA, I've been through my fair share of hip-hop gigs, but this crowd is unlike any I've ever seen. For one, the Lebanese crowd has an impeccable sense of fashion. Tonight, Beirut truly lives up to the term *Paris of the Middle East*. When 50 Cent hits the stage with "In Da Club," everyone's hands go up in the air and the crowd erupts. Nobody in Lebanon has ever seen one of the world's hottest rappers performing in their venue. Even till the last second before 50 Cent walked onto the stage, there were countless naysayers, believing this concert was just a scam and that such an enormous star would never show up in their country.

The gasps from the thousands of people facing the stage are audible, to 50 Cent's surprise. Seeing the energy of Beirut in front of him puts a genuine smile on his face.

During the performance, I turn away from the stage several times to look at Danny, who's smiling the whole time and rhythmically swaying to the beat of the songs.

"You did it, *habibi*," I scream into his ear.

"I told you, brother. Now we're crowned kings, and this is just the beginning."

The audience raps back the lyrics to the famous artist on the stage. I take a second to see the joy on everyone's faces and remember how this adventure started with a dream, an idea, and here we are, living it. The end of the show comes too fast. After the high-fives backstage and a quick chat like a true businessman, 50 Cent gets on his private jet and is off to his next endeavor.

For me, however, the best part of the night is about to come.

Heading over to SkyBar for its soft opening as the official after-party, we notice a complete madhouse outside. Thousands of people trying to get in, waving wads of cash to bribe the doormen. As the security makes way to escort Danny and our crew, I notice her like a morning sunflower, stoic against the forcefully moving island of spectators. Aleyna just has a way of glowing differently. Wearing a lacy little black dress with a diamond choker, she looks elegant and sultry at the same time.

I reach for her hand and pull her into our crew's small caravan, taking us to the only elevator going up to the SkyBar, the snazzy new rooftop lounge soaring among the clouds.

Seeing Danny, Sana and my friends squeezing themselves like sardines into the packed silver elevator, I say to my best friend, "Danny, I don't think it's safe. I don't see this shit going up. I'll wait for the next round."

He grabs my hand. "There's plenty of room. There's no next round. It'll be, like, hours. C'mon, you guys can fit. Move, move. Make room," he shouts at everyone to squeeze in together to accommodate Aleyna, Tarek and me.

As we're all forced inside the elevator too close for comfort, I see Tarek face to face for the first time since my "kidnapping." In a silent glance, it's acknowledged that there is no love lost between us, but Aleyna is more important than my pride.

Finally, the elevator trudges upward, making rattling sounds, like a struggling old tractor, as we manually push the doors together. Seeing the maximum occupancy posting inside and the shock in the eyes of the crowd outside, while we, in small jumpy increments, make it a few inches off the ground, I have little confidence in making it up to the club alive.

After a few long seconds of terror, the relief of getting off this elevator is maximized with the awe for the gorgeously designed nightclub with plush sofas, potted trees and twinkly lights. Situated on the rooftop with killer views of the Beirut waterfront and equipped with a state-of-the-art lighting and sound system, SkyBar is second to none in the Middle East. With the cool open sea air and luxurious seating, I forget where I am. It feels like I'm on the terrace at Pure Nightclub in Las Vegas, but a million times better.

As the night continues, the flashing lights and the amplified crowd roaring in a jamboree, Aleyna takes my hand to get on top of our VIP table and summons me to dance with her. She notices how uncomfortable it is for me and pulls me closer to shout in my ear, "Life is now, my love."

She dances and whirls like a dervish on the table, hypnotizing me to a drumbeat felt deep inside my body. Her smile, her sparkle, her scent in the air command my body to move like a Native American in some forgotten spiritual dance. Our auras dissolve into each other, surrounded by these beautiful people of light. It is in this place, this makeshift temple, at this moment, that I have a revelation. I am not only in love with Aleyna but also with Beirut. Never have I been encompassed by so many people engraved with a philosophy of *carpe diem*. I'm realizing that the definition of freedom we westerners treasure is all smoke and mirrors. Tomorrow is promised to no one, meanwhile most of us Americans spend our entire lives chasing after tomorrow. Putting our lives on hold because of the house, the car, the promotion that in the end will equate to nothing. No matter the amount of "things" you accumulate in life, we all leave with the same amount of nothing. Until now, the cup has never been full, but here in Beirut I've learned that having a cup is all you need because life will fill it if you let go and allow it. This is the true definition of freedom. I take Aleyna's hand as fireworks from the club erupt above our heads, lighting up the Mediterranean and her hazel eyes.

I kiss her and say, "Moments like this one... I want to live them with you." She pushes harder with her lips against mine, giving me her silent reply. From the corner of my eye, I see Danny and Sana kissing in their moment. I love this incredible city, its energy, its beauty, its buzz. I don't want to go home.

The amazing thing about living in the now is that it makes the time of happiness endlessly continue as it does for me for the next few weeks. From one night to the next, living like kings, we are reborn with our newfound freedom.

Inhaling the mystic hookah smoke with Danny on his chalet's balcony, we watch in awe as our Lebanese sun dives into the sea.

"Danny, what would you say if I told you I'm going to stay and marry Aleyna?" I ask out of the blue.

"Brother, I would say that's fucking amazing! I can't believe my boy and I are staying in my home country, getting married to two beautiful girls and living the dream."

I spill the beans to him, a little shy, "Danny, I bought two tickets to Cyprus leaving a few days after the Paul van Dyk concert. I want to ask her to marry me on those exquisite shores she keeps mentioning."

"Really? This is the first time in all these years I've known you that someone has successfully tamed you."

"I don't have a ring or a plan on how to stay here, but it's truly how I feel in my heart."

"Let me help you, *habibi*. The ring you can get at my mom's jewelry store and the plan is, since Abdul left to Qatar and Teddy to Dubai, you're going to be my right-hand man with the Shakira and Jay-Z concerts to help me build this company into a multi-million-dollar monster."

I'm touched and unsure what to say, exhaling the hookah smoke into the reddish sunset sky.

"By the way, I have the hundred grand for Sana's father in a bag in the closet and a ring. There's going to be the biggest, most lavish double wedding happening in Beirut this summer."

We both start laughing as the hookah's fragrant smoke drifts away in the warm evening breeze.

The Paul van Dyk concert was exactly what the white Buddha chemist must have had in mind when making those tiny pills. Aleyna and I rolled so hard that somehow, after the concert, we ended up in our little mountain getaway spot by the Baatara Gorge Waterfall again. Between the music and her flesh, the days became a blur.

One afternoon, lying on the bed naked eating watermelon slices, I say to her, "My love, I have a surprise for you."

"I have a surprise for you too. It's almost your birthday." She cuddles into my shoulder, tracing little hearts on my bare chest. I feel an overwhelming love for her.

"We really have to get back to Jounieh to catch our flight tomorrow morning. We can stay at Danny's and leave together to the airport."

"*Airport?* I'll text Tarek to make arrangements. You know he must go everywhere I go. I don't want to make my father raving mad like last time. You truly surprise me, my love."

"Good, I'm glad."

"Living in the moment? Look at you, Ashe. Almost a Beiruti," she says with a smile as she takes a big bite of the watermelon.

Arriving at Danny's chalet that night, the scene is filled with tawla which is the Middle Eastern name for backgammon, laughs, music and a feast of homemade food. With Abdul gone, my room is private just for Aleyna and me. It's a gorgeous July evening, the sultry breeze carries the intoxicating scents of cedar and salty sea air through my window. Lying in bed, we can't resist embracing each other through the star-filled night. Through our open window the Mediterranean Sea listens to our whispers in the night and as much as I want to live in this moment forever, with her diamond ring in my pocket, I can't wait till tomorrow. Looking out onto the reflections of millions of stars on the dark sea, we fall asleep.

Just as we drift off, I'm startled awake by the loud banging at my door. I fly out of bed, grabbing my clothes, confused and worried we might have overslept and we're going to miss our flight. I open the door and I see Danny's ghostly face.

"What time is it, *habibi*? Can you drive us to the airport?" I say, thinking that it must be really late into the morning as I start putting my clothes on.

"No, no, Ashe. You both need to come see this," he replies, pointing at the TV in the living room where Anwar, Michelle and the maids, all huddled with horror on their faces, are watching.

"I don't have time for this. We're going to miss our flight to Cyprus. Can you please take Aleyna and me to the airport? We'll be ready in five minutes," I say, as Aleyna's already dressed and getting our bags.

"Ashe, you're not going anywhere," he says with a bone-chilling calmness in his voice.

"What are you talking about? I have the tickets right here." I wave two Middle Eastern Airlines tickets in front of his face.

"You need to come see this!"

"I can't. We have to make it to Cyprus. Remember how important this trip is?" I say, winking in disbelief at why my best friend's acting so strange. Reluctantly walking closer to the TV, I stop, paralyzed in dread at what I see.

Danny puts his hand on my shoulder. "Ashe, see, you can't leave. No one can leave. There's no airport anymore."

EXTREME TO EXTREME

"Wandering off past the zenith of my life."

My euphoria of falling in love with this ancient land slowly unravels, second by second, as I watch the CNN news in panic. The Beirut-Rafic Hariri International Airport's runway has been decimated into a pile of smoke and rubble we can clearly see at a distance from our front balcony. The news anchor goes over the events. Apparently, two Israeli soldiers were kidnapped on the Lebanese border by the Hezbollah, the powerful Iran-backed Shia paramilitary group. And so in a flash of retaliation, to prevent the Hezbollah from smuggling the hostages out of the country, the Israeli military bombed overnight not only the airport but the main bridges and the Beirut-Damascus Highway leading out of Lebanon, tightening off the air, land and sea blockade. The number of Lebanese casualties rises minute by minute.

Amid the unfolding terror attack and death count, Israel's Defense Forces Chief of Staff Dan Halutz told journalists: "If the soldiers are not returned, we will turn Lebanon's clock back 20 years." His statement strikes me as scripted but full of venom.

I look at Aleyna's eyes brimming with tears. Michelle is losing her cool, while Anwar and Danny are sitting in uneasy silence. It feels like somebody has to say something, but we have all lost our voices.

Everyone was in such an ebullient mood the night before—and in an instant, everything turned to shit.

That morning, JULY 12TH, 2006, looking at my friends' distraught faces as they realize their lives have been upended, I'm shocked and can't quite believe this is happening. I came for a summer of adventure and found myself in a country ripped apart by violence and tipped into war overnight.

You were right, Rodger, I grew up sheltered in Los Angeles.

If I saw war or famine on TV, it almost wasn't real. I could simply change the channel and forget about it. There were no fires or rockets flying for targets outside my window. The glimpse of safety I felt here will never return now.

Aleyna clenches my hand and says her father has summoned her: she has to go home. The fatalistic look on her face sends quivers into my heart, but the weight of the diamond ring in my pocket grows heavy, reminding me what could have been.

After Tarek hastily arrives to pick up Aleyna, Danny tries to reassure us. "Guys, this happens all the time here. Don't worry, in a couple of days it'll blow over."

Starving for more information, the four of us sit glued to the TV. When CNN is on a commercial break, Anwar frantically switches the channels looking for more news coverage. When he lands on the Al Jazeera news channel, we see a different side of the truth. Instead of the number of victims we see in western media, we are shown their faces and stories. It's raw, bloody and devastating. A one-month-old baby girl and her entire family are gone underneath the rubble, where their home once stood. As we watch the Al Jazeera news coverage in suspense, we see that most of the casualties aren't military but innocent civilians. Their only fault is being in the wrong place at the wrong time. My heart breaks for these beautiful people who welcomed me, a foreigner, with open arms.

As we watch the images of devastation, people trapped beneath the rubble, crying women and children soaked in blood, tears start rolling down my cheeks.

"And they call us terrorists," Anwar vents his frustration before changing the channel to a station I have never seen before. "This is the real shit. This is Hezbollah's news station, Al-Manar."

"What are you talking about? The terrorists have their own news station?" I ask, shocked.

"They are *not* terrorists, Ashe," Danny shoots down my uninformed reductionist clichés about the Middle East and blows away my western preconceptions. "That's the American lie they fed you to believe. Hezbollah are freedom fighters for Lebanon. They love and die for this country. We may not see eye to eye, but no one really does in this part of the world."

Within a few days the Israelis bomb the satellite station, but it still continues broadcasting. On the Al-Manar channel, the spokesperson for the Hezbollah, which literally means the Party of God, paints a completely different picture of the conflict, saying that the dead are martyrs, that the resistance will rise and fight to free the Lebanese people from Israel's brutality and oppression. He claims that the Israeli soldiers were doing missions inside of Lebanon when they were captured, and Hezbollah's goal is now to do a prisoner exchange for their countrymen in Israel's prison.

His words twist my preconceived ideas of the conflict. Where is the truth? I see the dead bodies, but with a flip of a channel, I'm being told contrasting realities of how and why their lives were taken.

As night falls, Danny tries to cheer us up with a lavish meal, but we can only muster a few bites. It feels like The Last Supper as we all sit around the table glumly, Danny and I quietly staring toward the windows, Michelle sipping on her wine for medication and Anwar cradling the hookah.

With Abdul gone back home to Qatar and Aleyna whisked away to her palatial compound, the four of us are holed up in the chalet, fearful and restless. There are no phone calls tonight inviting us to glamorous parties or clubs. There are no fancy cars speeding through the empty streets. As I look out from the balcony, the dark stores are boarded up and the restaurants are deserted. The only break in the deadening silence is an intermittent glare and zipping of distant Israeli airstrikes hitting targets south of us. The southern coastline, once vibrant with shimmering city lights, is now pitch-black. Out of the darkness of the mountains come hundreds of missiles heading toward Israel, weaving a tapestry of death all over the night sky.

The display of lights and explosions paint a hypnotizing picture we cannot turn away from. Our distance from the fiery sky and Danny's reassurance give us a sense of invulnerability, enough to close our eyes and dream an end to this conflict.

Morning comes at a high price. The TV, once again the focus of all of our attention, recalls the night's casualties. I look out the window and notice that the birds are not singing, as if they have suffocated on the smoky skies over Lebanon. From the balcony, I can see the rising plumes of reddish smoke and the acrid smell of sulfurous chemicals. I walk up to Danny, whose face has changed overnight. Pale with fear, he tries to keep his composure in front of us, making coffee as if nothing happened.

"Danny, do you think we're safe here?" I ask naively.

"Of course, *habibi*. We're on the Christian side of Lebanon. This war is between Hezbollah and Israel," he says in his typically stoic, matter-of-fact way, hiding his anxiety and fear.

"That smoke over there. Isn't that where Sana lives?" I ask, fearing the worst.

"Yes, Ashe. I haven't heard from her. I pray she evacuated before last night's airstrikes," he says, tears misting his sad brown eyes.

"I was going to propose to Aleyna today in Cyprus." I take out the diamond ring from my pocket. Danny looks at it and smiles wearily as he hands me a cup of black coffee. "But I haven't heard from her yet. I'm sure they're both okay."

"Ashe, our Lebanese dreams have been scorched overnight. I just received a flood of emails. Shakira, Jay-Z, Erick Morillo, everyone has cancelled, and Erick kept his deposit. I lost so much money. It's going to take years to get the world's trust back in Beirut."

"I can't imagine what our next steps should be. What are we going to do?" I ask, terrified of the unknown.

Michelle dashes into the living room, shouting at the top of her voice, "Guys, something large is in the sea and heading toward us. Come... come, look!" She pulls me by the arm to the coast-facing balcony and Danny and Anwar rush over behind us. The sea water is parting with a force created by what looks like a giant humpback whale.

"What the fuck is that?!" Anwar says, looking worried. "It's heading straight for the naval base."

Suddenly the giant black object emerges from the sea and what appears to be antennae rise above the water.

"Holy shit! That's a submarine! I can see the periscope!" Danny yells in fright, but before he can add anything else, two platform anti-aircraft machine guns from the mountains fire thousands of rounds at the submarine. The speed and quantity of the bullets create lightning-like lines connecting the mountains to the submarine. It almost looks beautiful, if not for the terrifying sound that cracks my skin. Still pushing forward through the water, unfazed by the rain of bullets, it fully emerges and comes to a complete stop.

We stand together on the balcony in disbelief as two small hatches on the Israeli submarine blow open.

"Go, go, go! Inside!" Danny shouts.

Stirring with feelings of hopelessness and shock, none of us can move, like deer in the headlights. In an intense moment of horror, we watch the submarine launching numerous rockets into our once tranquil turquoise sky. Michelle screams like a gunshot before a race and we all sprint toward the front door, but it's too late. As the rockets hit their targets, we are thrown to the ground by the overpowering g-force.

I feel the floor shudder and the windows rattle. Everything, from the couch to the paintings in the chalet, lifts for a second and is thrown back down on the floor, like the powerful pre-dawn earthquake that shook us from our sleep back home in LA in 1994. The shattering glass dances in the sunlight before hitting the ground.

I land hard on my chest. Pinned to the shaking floor, as if the devil himself has put his foot on top of my back, I see a shimmer of broken glass on the floor and trails of cement dust fall from the ceiling cracking above our heads while the whole building sways from the blast. Short-lived screams fill the air as the neighboring building collapses into a deadly silence.

Heavy with thoughts of Aleyna, home and God, unable to rise from the ground, I squint my eyes open.

Through the speckles of falling dust, I see Rodger Henderson, sitting in his yoga pose with a cigarette in his hand, smiling. I ask him one last question: *"Is my vessel filled now?"*

MURMUR OF THE LAND

"Hope is sown in the fields of war."

The scent of death creeps in and fills my nostrils. Plastered with cement dust, my lungs remember how to exhale as I cough out the fear. Slowly rising back on our feet, we notice Michelle is still on the floor. The blast flung her across the room, and she is lying there like a broken doll. Her blazing-red hair stuccoed with dust veils, her unmoving body in the corner of the hallway.

We rush to her and Danny slowly shakes her. "Michelle! Michelle... are you all right?"

She coughs. "I'm fine. Gimme a second. My ears can't stop ringing," she replies, hugging herself in the fetal position.

"Michelle, let us help you up. We need to get out of the building right now! It may collapse from the damage," Danny says gently but with a sense of urgency.

"Fine. I'm coming." Apart from a few tiny cuts on her arms from the shattered glass, she is unharmed. Shaking the dust and debris from her hair, she gets up on her own and we all slowly head down the broken, graveled staircase. It's a familiar feeling of being a foreigner in my body as I struggle with each step. Only that this is not the mask class at CalArts, this is war.

Outside, Danny evaluates the condition of the building and his car. Our apartment block, aside from a few smashed windows, cracked door frames and mangled balcony railings, hasn't been damaged much, while the building next door has been completely flattened. Taking in the devastation and the desperate, bloodied faces, the emotion of the moment paralyzes me. Michelle, in a daze, walks off to the shoreline and sits down on a large seaside boulder. She looks to the left at the burning pile of structures that just minutes ago used to be the Lebanese naval base. Staring numbly into the distance, she looks like she's a step away from a complete meltdown.

The submarine is gone, but the pain has just arrived. The silence of the land is broken by woeful screams. I barely have time to process what's happening when a blue pickup truck speeds past through the street toward the collapsed building. Guided by our better angels, Anwar and I run after it, crunching through broken glass and debris. On the other side of the street, a handful of people are digging with their bare hands through the piles of gravel, hopeful for survivors. Without hesitation or instruction, Anwar and I join them. The weight of the stone presses against my numb hands as we look for any signs of life in the rubble.

My eyes pause at a man searching frantically 15 feet in front of me. The blood coming from his ear coalesces at his jawline as he bellows, "Zahra! Zahra! Zahra!"

He collapses to his knees and starts throwing the stones away faster and faster and we all rush to his side to help. A small bare foot sticking out from underneath the gravel gives us hope. When he pulls a little girl from the mound of concrete, his howling is conjoined by the women gathered at the side of the street. He holds his daughter's bloodied body tight in his arms while someone covers her with a tattered Lebanese flag. The father whispers something to her departed soul as he looks up at the sky with tears falling down his dusty, greyish face. He tenderly swaddles her lifeless remains in the Lebanese flag while her mother leans over them, screaming in despair.

With a look of deep grief on their faces, they both huddle over the dead child, saying her name again and again.

I feel overwhelmed by the violence and injustice, painfully aware that there is little I can do to help. Choking up, I try to breathe out the torment and my eyes well up. I shield my face with my arms and bow my head down in an attempt to escape from the sorrow. The mother's cries bring me to my knees as I look down at the burnt ground and see the scattered photos of the happy families who once lived in this now-collapsed apartment building. This is an emotional landscape I have never seen in America. I do not see one dead "terrorist" in this rubble. All I see is the blood of children. There is no escape. I can't hold back the tears anymore. They wet the bloody pieces of stone and pictures beneath me.

It's indescribably heartbreaking looking at the people and the neighborhoods I was just getting to know being destroyed so brutally.

Anwar puts his hand on my shoulder. "Brother, they need a hand over here. You okay to help?" He waves toward the blue truck parked next to the building that is surrounded by people struggling to load the injured onto its cargo bed.

"I'm coming," I reply, wiping tears from my face, trying to get myself together inside.

As the frantic search for survivors is underway, we walk over to help load a handful of people with multiple injuries. Open fractures wrapped with scarves, head lacerations and an elderly man breathing what seems his last breaths, praying silently. After we fill the little blue truck with dying and injured people, a man in his 40s, soaked in blood, whether his own or someone else's, taps the side of the truck and it speeds away toward the local hospital. A thin trail of blood falls to the ground from the open tailgate.

It is here at this moment that I see something inconceivable to my American mind. Strangers marching through every corner of Beirut's streets to help those they do not know. In times of conflict and strife, the Lebanese unite. I read somewhere once that in the darkest of times comes the brightest of lights.

The light of the Beirutis is blinding.

As an Angeleno, I vividly remember the LA Riots of 1992. Being 15 years old, pulled out of high school and cooped up at home, day after day I watched LA burning on TV. When the police pulled back their positions in South Central LA, the rioters, looters and arsonists were unhinged, destroying our beautiful city. In the end, they damaged over a billion dollars' worth of property, killing 64 people and injuring thousands. I remember that the National Guard had to step in to put a stop to the unrest. So naturally, I always believed that chaos will ensue if there is no law and order to police citizens. Not in Beirut. Today my vessel fills with hope for humanity as I see, with no police in sight, no looters, no arsonists taking advantage of the surrounding mayhem.

All I see in Beirut during these grim times are angels.

After several hours of digging through the wreckage and finding no one else, I hear Danny screaming for us to come back to the chalet. Bewildered and emotionally drained, Anwar and I walk over, covered in dirt and blood from head to toe.

"My God! We have power and our building survived," Danny says, amazed. "Come, we don't know how long it will last. The landline still works. Let's make some calls and send emails and see if we can get the fuck out of here."

Before I walk up the splintered staircase, I notice Michelle still sitting on the same boulder by the shore. She hasn't moved in hours. Danny walks up to her and says something I cannot hear. Michelle gets up and hugs Danny before they walk back to join Anwar and me.

In the relative calm of our chalet, with the power and lights back on, Danny immediately calls his father, an ex-general of the Lebanese army, and they exchange words in Arabic I can't understand.

The first call I make is to Aleyna. "Hello." Her seraphic voice on the other end gives me such immense relief that I pause, unable to say anything for a second as she repeats, "Hello?"

"*Hayete*, I didn't think I was going to hear your voice again," I say, still in shock. The cracks in the ceiling remind me of how close death came to taking me today.

"My love, I can't leave right now but I'm safe, and I'll come get you tomorrow. Stay alive, my heart," she replies as I hurry to get off the phone so that my friends have time to call their loved ones before the power goes out again.

Michelle is increasingly agitated and erratic, a barely contained explosion. While she calls her father, I discover the internet is still working and so I email my mother.

When Michelle gets off the phone, she says to us, "Fuck this shit! I'm outta here." She looks scared and frantic, rushing into her room and erratically shoving her designer clothes and other belongings into her small carry-on.

"Michelle, what are you doing?" Anwar asks.

"I'm fucking leaving, dude," she replies, pissed that he even would question her judgment, "getting out of this shitty war before we all die here."

Danny tries to reason with her. "Where are you going to go? Every road leading out of Lebanon most likely has been bombed."

"I'm gonna get in a fucking taxi and pay them whatever the fuck they want to get me to Syria. There, I can buy a plane ticket and fly home. Anyone wanna come with me? I'll pay for everything. I have the money." She pauses packing, swiveling her head around for an answer.

Anwar and Danny leave the room without responding, making gestures to imply how insane her idea sounds.

As I'm helping her zip up the bursting luggage, she takes my hand and asks, tearing up, "Ashe, come with me out of this hell. We don't belong here."

"My heart won't let me, but you go... get out of this fucking chaos." I give her an encouraging hug before her arduous journey. "I know if anyone can make it home, it's you. You're a fiery redhead, so fight hard and when you make it home and if I don't, please tell my family I love them," I say to her and she hugs me tighter as though she won't ever see me again.

A part of me worries about her, a lone woman traveling through a war zone, but somehow I know she will be fine. She has a tough New York brassiness about her.

She wipes her tears away and grabs her bag. Like a super-model walking down the runway, unstoppable, Michelle walks down the hallway, out the door and hops into the first taxi that stops.

"Come on, Ashe," Danny says to me, putting his shoes on in a hurry. "Michelle will be okay. Let's go. We're going to my parents' for dinner and to ask my father for help to get us out of the country. He was one of the highest-ranking generals in the Lebanese military. He'll know what to do."

With the streets nearly empty of people and cars, driving past shelled-out buildings, wrecked shopfronts and shattered houses is like being in some post-apocalyptic movie. When we arrive at Danny's parents' house, his mother, a very well-dressed and vibrant woman in her 70s with a kind face, greets us warmly. She welcomes me and Anwar with a hug and a kiss on both cheeks. Glancing around the spacious house, beautifully decorated with mid-century modernist furniture that looks as though little has changed since the 1960s, you wouldn't know there was a war going on. Most of the surfaces and shelves are filled with books, family photos, flowers and other shiny artifacts of a life well lived. Without asking if we're hungry, she immediately leads us to the dinner table covered in a mountain of food, steaming plates of flatbreads and falafel, smoky baba ghanoush, lemony hummus, tabbouleh, stuffed grape leaves, green salad drizzled in olive oil and lemon juice and stacks of baklava.

Danny's father—a stern old gent with slicked-back, silvery hair, a clean-shaven face and a serious brow—is sitting at the head of the table. He looks like an older, fleshier version of Danny. A man of few words, he gives us a firm handshake but gets up to hug his son before we all sit down for dinner.

Amid this atmosphere of hunch-shouldered silence and wariness, I grasp for something to say. Seeing the empty plate and seat to the right of me, I tell her, "Mrs. Bitar, before you bring out more food, our friend Michelle has left and won't be joining us."

She gives me an incredulous look and turns to her son with an exaggerated sigh. "Danny, why did you bring your American friend to Lebanon?"

She isn't joking.

"He does not know death the way we are forced to know her. She sits at our table. The plate reminds us of those she took too soon from us," she says introspectively. "In Lebanon, we die of bullets and bombs like you in America die of cancer and old age."

"Mom, this is why we're here. I came to ask for Dad's help to get my friends back to the US," Danny says respectfully.

Between cigarette puffs, his father speaks in Arabic and everyone listens. I'm listening intently even though I can't understand a word. He sounds serious and concerned. The weary look on my friends' faces is not encouraging.

Danny glances at me and explains, "My father says there's no getting out safely. As long as the Israeli fighter jets blanket the sky and intermittently bomb Lebanon at their own discretion, we're stuck here. The Israeli naval and air blockade is too formidable."

His parents, who've lived through decades of almost ceaseless conflict with Israel, Syria and other volatile Arab nations, take the long view that this war like the others will end sometime. This sudden violent chaos and instability is a constant backdrop to their lives. I can't begin to imagine how they emerged from it without being subsumed by bitterness.

I look at Danny with a sense of resignation. The beautiful food in front of us reminds me I haven't eaten all day, even though I don't feel hungry.

At the end of the night, we get back to the chalet after the somber dinner. Our stomachs are full, but our souls are empty. The phone rings and we all rush to it, thinking it might be Michelle.

Danny answers hopefully, "Hello, Michelle? Oh... hi, Johnny." He stays on the phone for several minutes, listening to whatever Johnny is saying. When he hangs up, the news traumatizes us. Apparently, Johnny's beautiful coastal paradise resort we visited was bombed. It's gone, along with his dreams. Danny tells us he sounded suicidal, but he talked him off the ledge and invited him to stay with us, although Johnny declined.

We all sat on the couch in shell-shocked silence. All our dreams are going up in smoke. Such an unbelievable thing. Only days before, Beirut was a place where everything seemed possible; now it is all violence and darkness.

It turns out that the Israelis were bombing not just areas with a Hezbollah presence but roads, seaports, power plants across the country. Israel had only just left southern Lebanon four years before with their tails between their legs after the brutality of the 18-year occupation. And now they were using the taking of hostages to exact revenge and tear the country apart again.

Danny turns to me and says, "Amira's factories are in the same area as Johnny's resort."

I look at him, stunned, thinking surely someone as monied and well connected as Amira would've already fled the country in a private jet.

"I'm going to call her," I say, picking up the phone.

The phone rings and rings. Finally, when I'm about to hang up, Amira answers. She tells me through sobs that the Israeli military wrongfully bombed her multimillion-dollar factories. Factories that are supplying steel barracks for the US armed forces in Iraq. The irony of war. I try to console her by saying she can rebuild with insurance reimbursements. She breaks out in an audible laugh, explaining to me that there is no war insurance. That neither Israel nor Lebanon will rebuild her factories; it's always a burden on the innocent people to start over in this part of the world. We wish each other farewell as Danny waves at me to get off the phone.

"I have the most amazing plan, boys. We're going to get out of here," he says, smiling, rushing to the phone as he dials a number.

"What's your *plan*, Danny?" Anwar asks with a hint of sarcasm.

"Watch this!" Danny puts the phone on speaker while he waits for someone to answer.

"Hello?" a familiar man's voice answers.

"Hey, Chris. It's your boy DB. I have Ashe and Anwar here. We're all US citizens and we need to get out of Lebanon. Can you help?" Danny confidently cuts to the chase.

"Oh, hey, guys. What happened to Michelle?" Chris asks curiously.

"She left today for Syria in a taxi."

"Man, I had a feeling that girl was bat-shit crazy. I hope she makes it. Many people haven't. All major roads leading out of Lebanon are heavily targeted areas. Hopefully she'll drive through the desert and stay off the main highways."

"Can you help us get out, Chris?" Anwar asks impatiently from the couch.

"Hey, Anwar, good to hear you're okay, but I'm sorry, guys. My hands are tied."

"What do you mean, Chris? We're US citizens, isn't the American Embassy here to help us?" Danny asks, confused.

"All right, guys, I'm going to level with you, but you can't repeat what I'm about to say. We've petitioned up the chain of command on the behest of the 25,000 US citizens trapped here. The response was 'fuck 'em, they know we're currently at war in the Middle East, and they shouldn't be there.' So, guys, I don't know what to tell you other than stay put and eventually the US military will come get you."

Chris shocks us. We all exchange stunned glances.

"Hi, Chris, it's Ashe. When, bud? When do you think they will come to get us?"

"Hey, Ashe. The US coming for you all depends on the public pressure on politicians. Could be days or could be months, no one knows. I'm out of here, so you boys take care of each other and watch each other's backs. I can't say anything else. This is our last communication. I have to go. Good luck," he says and hangs up without waiting for our reply.

The disconnected line beeps loudly on the speakerphone. Danny, Anwar and I stand looking at each other in fearful disbelief. The phone suddenly stops beeping as the power goes out once more and we light candles. A routine occurrence for us at this time of the night is sitting in the candlelit living room, listening to the rockets launched toward Israel by Hezbollah from different positions in the mountains, and feeling the bombs drop on Lebanon from Israeli jets.

One evening, waiting for the horrific sounds to commence, the stifling silence surprises us. There are no rockets in the air or the buzz of jets overhead, terrorizing us.

The unnerving stillness of the night in Lebanon brings me to say, "This is it. This is how death comes. Silent in the night. Something bad is going to happen."

"Why did they stop bombing?" Anwar asks, confused.

"My dad was right," Danny answers, staring at the dancing flame of the candle on the coffee table. "The phantoms of war have come back to haunt us."

Then suddenly, in the distance, we hear a rhythmic sound of a helicopter coming from the seaside. We run out onto the balcony facing the sea. Out of the blackness of the water, two large transport helicopters emerge into our horizon. Flying over our building, the floor vibrates vigorously as we feel the air move by their powerful propellers.

"It's the United States Marines!" Anwar shouts excitedly. "They're here! They're here to save us! We're going home! It's over!"

We jump with joy like little kids, hugging each other, and then we all rush to the other balcony to see the location of their landing.

"I think they're going to the American Embassy," Danny says as we observe the large black helicopters, which typically carry armed troops, land near the Embassy compound.

Still, Anwar remains calm, convinced that once they rescue the Embassy staff and other officials, they will return for us.

The night once again falls disconcertingly silent. Before we can make sense of what's going on or decide what we should do, the sky roars again with the sound of the helicopters flying right past us.

"Wait a minute, they just got here! Why are they leaving without us?" Anwar says, frustrated, shattering our glint of hope.

"They're evacuating the Embassy personnel," Danny replies with disappointment in his voice.

In a state of panicked confusion, I look around the city from our balcony and can see other shadows staring at the disappearing helicopters. In unison, we rush to the shore-facing balcony and watch our hopes fly away into the blackness of the Mediterranean Sea.

Anwar looks gutted and scared. "Do you think they're coming back?"

"No, Anwar," Danny replies somberly. "That was it. They got who they came for. We don't matter. Our own government has deserted us in a war zone."

Danny's words hit like darts in my heart as I watch the shadows on the balconies retreat into their darkness. In the end, thousands of American citizens like us are left stranded. There's no ability to switch this frightful channel when the rockets start falling again.

If anyone can restrain the Israelis, it's the Americans who paid for their arsenal and, if not sanctioned their actions, rarely condemned them. I worry that once the American officials and other foreign nationals are evacuated by their governments, the bombing is likely to get worse. The reality sets in: hope is a currency we can no longer afford.

STATE OF EMOTIONAL EMERGENCY

"A beggar who made a deal with God."

Nestled closely in the living room of Danny's chalet, we're surrounded by the flickering of candlelight and prayers for survival. With the long and frequent blackouts, we learn what times the power cuts usually happen and quickly adapt to living under siege. When the electricity goes out and the generator isn't working, we light candles, eat dinner and sit together, telling stories to escape our nightly torment. Beirut is disturbingly silent, without even an electrical hum from the transformers. The streets remain paralyzed and deserted after many of our neighbors, those who weren't wounded or killed, fled to the mountains. It's so quiet we can hear one of our candles burn out.

As Danny lights up a match to ignite a new candle, the flames of rockets heading toward Israel blaze the sky once more.

The rolling thunder of Israeli jets flying over the rocket plumes bombarding our city steals the silence away as the smoke from explosions fills the air.

The ceasefire, if there was one, is short-lived.

"What happened? Why are they bombing us again?" Anwar says, his voice breaking.

Watching the white tails of the rockets shoot out from the cedar mountains and usher in my 29th birthday, my mind swells at the thought that it might be my last. *What the hell was I thinking coming here, dodging Israeli bombs and living like a fugitive?*

Danny and Anwar, emotionally exhausted, slouch deep into sofa, silently staring out the windows at the billowing smoke and mushroom clouds in the not-too-far distance.

To break the tension, I say, "Well, we've just witnessed the power of the United States."

Anwar looks at me confused as I continue, "All of our lives we're told that the United States is the most powerful country in the world, but we've never seen it till now. The war was indisputably paused on both sides just so our Embassy could be safely evacuated. If that's not power, then tell me what is? No other country could do that."

"So much power, huh?" Anwar says, irked. "But somehow not enough power to stop the slaughter of the innocent."

Danny looks at us with sorrow in his eyes. "Power differs from desire, Anwar. There simply is no desire to stop this suffering." He points to the missiles crowding the night sky.

These monstrous nights become a habitual occurrence. Only in the daylight are we spared their wrath. For now, the war seems to happen primarily late at night. We see some of our neighbors packing and leaving, while others spend their days fixing and patching up the damage to their wrecked homes amid the large dirt wastelands. There's a universal exhaustion on everyone's face because no one can sleep at night anymore.

It takes Aleyna several days to come to me. It's a beautiful summer morning, if one can ignore the south of Beirut covered in dust and smoke from last night's missile attacks. Aleyna's gentle knock at our chalet's door fills me with elation, a feeling that I almost forgot.

"My love," she whispers, burying her face into my chest as we embrace the instant I open the door. I'm unable to move from the weight of the moment.

"I was so worried about you. Never leave me again, *hayete*," I whisper back and kiss the top of her blonde head.

"I won't, I promise. I'm taking you with me. Your friends are welcome to come too," she says, looking at our surprised faces. "We have to escape to the mountains, where it's safe, but we have to go now to make it there before the sun goes down and the bombings start again." She takes my hand, guiding me to my room to pack.

Danny follows us. "*Habibi*, I can't go. I haven't heard from Sana in a few days and I promised I'd be here for her, at the chalet. I have to stay."

"I'll stay with Danny. You two go ahead," Anwar shouts from the living room. "I'd rather be here in case these US helicopters come back to get us."

We drive out of the city, taking the backroads up to the hills to avoid the bombed-out highways and main roads. Sitting in the backseat of her car, Aleyna and I hold on to each other tight. Her driver speeds through the winding mountain roads, while Tarek looks up in the sky for any sign of Israeli fighter jets. Just before dusk we arrive at a hotel hidden away in the forested mountains. Aleyna scoots to the edge of the backseat when she sees her friends and their families gathered by the dozens, awaiting her arrival. Their cars line the entire street outside the hotel. They greet her with hugs and tears of relief as I follow her to the front desk.

For the past several months, it would always escape my mind that I was actually dating a billionaire. Aleyna never flaunted her wealth in front of me or anyone else. The dinners were simple, the dates were inexpensive, her clothes were never flashy. Not once did she make me feel undeserving of her love. But at this moment, I feel the magnitude of her wealth and the measure of her heart.

"I would like to rent out the entire hotel, please," Aleyna says confidently, handing over her credit card to the front-desk receptionist. The lady glances at the name on the card and immediately nods her head and starts handing her room keys.

One by one, Aleyna's friends and their families receive their keys, as she tells them, "You'll be safe here. Stay as long as you need to. You're welcome."

I glance over and see the pride on Tarek's face. He knows he guards an angel.

For the first time in weeks, we hear no bombs, see no fires and feel no tremors from our balcony. It creates an illusion that the war does not exist. The same comfortable ignorance I felt in America.

Looking out onto the starry horizon, Aleyna quietly walks up to me and places her hand on my chest. "Ashe, you don't have to speak. I feel the earthquakes in your heart."

The touch of her hand reminds me of how I longed for her closeness. Lying beside her, scared to dream of a life together after the war but not scared enough to love. There are walls in every man's soul that are hard to tear down. Having brushed against mortality in Beirut, I finally have no more walls.

"Aleyna, I don't know what will happen to us in this war, but at this moment, I just want to love you. The Beiruti way," I say, looking into her fiery brown eyes.

"The Beiruti way is the only way we have, my love," she replies and kisses me passionately.

That night, our bodies become one, a memory etched in our souls forever, like the words on a tombstone.

The bliss is all too short-lived. By the time the rays of morning light touch Aleyna's bare, sun-flushed skin, her phone rings. Her father summons her back home. He hints that he has negotiated a way out of this hell.

Leaving her friends and their families at the hotel, we rush back to Beirut, only to see the devastation on our way down from the mountains. The beige apartment buildings are bullet-pock-marked and peppered with smoke from the blasts of missiles. Everything crumbled like toppled dominoes. The skeletons of cars are melted to the ground like burned marshmallows. War fills the air with a sickly sulfur-like smell. The buildings where Lebanese families once lived are now just dark, empty massive holes. We slept through their pain. You hear nothing. Even the birds know this land is dying.

I'm relieved to see Danny and Anwar in one piece at the chalet, although saddened once more that Aleyna had to return home and I don't know when I'll see her again.

"We missed you, brother," Danny says sadly and gives me a tight hug.

"We came back, but I have a feeling Aleyna and her family are getting out of here," I say to my friends.

"I'm not sure what to do. I haven't heard from Sana. I suspect she's in hiding with her family. Johnny never showed up or called and Michelle... I don't know, no word from her either."

Anwar fills me in, "Still nothing on the news about the US coming back to get us out of here. We got bombed last night... a lot. It's getting much worse. I think it's time for us to explore other options of getting out of Lebanon, if there even are any."

"I don't know how much longer we can survive here," I say, shaken.

Danny looks at us, then looks out the window at the scarred city and, with red-rimmed glassy eyes, says, "This once-vibrant city is now dead."

The weight of his words hangs on us through the day till the dusk. That night, ideas of escape brew in our minds. As we sit huddled in the darkness, the violent escalation disables our bodies but not our thoughts.

A vigorous knock at the door breaks the suspense.

Danny flies off the sofa to answer it, saying one word, "Sana?" As the door squeaks open, he says in surprise, "Oh my God! What are you doing here? How did you get here? Come in... come in!"

Anwar and I rush to the door, curious to find out who is the brave spirit who weathered the storm of missiles outside. The silhouette in the dark hallway comes into focus as we get closer and I catch the glimpse of golden hair underneath a black hoodie.

Aleyna's eyes well up as I grasp her scared, shivering body in my arms. My friends wipe their eyes in a tearful moment. I lift her up and, in a tight grasp, carry her to my room. Sitting her on the edge of my bed, I kneel in front of her as she leans in and rests her head on my forehead.

"Aleyna, what are you doing here? You could've been killed," I say quietly as the thought of her risking her life to see me makes my eyes water.

She gently wipes away the hot, streaming tears off my cheeks. "My life was worth a possibility of another night with you."

"But how did you get here?" I ask, stunned, kissing the scar on her finger.

She cups my face with her hands and, looking into my red teary eyes, and tells me how she snuck out of the compound.

"My heart tore out of my chest, so I had to follow it," she explains in breathless rasps. "I paid a man to wait in a car outside my family's compound. I climbed over the side wall and in his speeding car I rolled down the backseat window, so my prayers were louder for God to hear than the explosions. We were the only car on the road. I had to come, my love, because it's the last night we'll have together in Beirut. My family is leaving tomorrow for Germany."

I take her left hand and caress her ring finger, where her engagement ring would have been. "I love you so much, *hayete*. This is the most extraordinary act of love I've ever received or could even imagine being worthy of."

She kisses my lips. "Hold me, hold me close all night and tell me a story that takes me back to the Bread and Brown, where I fell in love with my wet, dreamy American."

With the balcony windows open, like fireworks, the flashes of orange and red light up our faces throughout the night. We cradle each other as the land shakes under the mushroom clouds of smoke. We lay beneath death's gaze as the waves crash on the boulders below.

Seizing every second of time, lost in each other's arms, we are shaken back to reality by the banging on the front door early in the morning.

Again, Danny springs to the door, hoping it's Sana. "Ashe, it's for you," he says, sounding disappointed.

Aleyna and I quickly get dressed and rush to the living room to see Tarek standing there, looking pissed off.

"Tarek, it's my fault. Please don't be mad at her," I say, caught off guard by his frowning face.

"Mr. Ashe, this is not the first time Miss Aleyna has eluded me. She's very smart, but this time it was a dangerous move," he says in a monotone voice.

"You understand, don't you, Tarek?" Aleyna says to him, clasping my hand.

"Yes, Miss Aleyna, and so does your father. Time to go." Tarek opens the front door, waiting for her to follow him. She lets go of my hand and her eyes mist.

As she walks toward the door, Tarek turns to me. "You too, Mr. Ashe. I was instructed to bring both of you."

Aleyna stops and looks back at me with a cautious hope in her eyes.

Passing the guarded security gate into Aleyna's family compound, Tarek drives us to the back of the main house. The acres of manicured landscape adorned with marble statues, which still escape the hand of war, welcome us. I notice people gathered in the middle of the massive green lawn next to a black military helicopter.

Aleyna's father strides over to us with a concerned look in his eyes, saying something to his daughter in Arabic.

Aleyna hesitantly lets go of my hand once again and kisses me on the cheek. "I'll see you in a second, my love."

As she walks unhurriedly, the helicopter's main rotor beats

slowly and her sunlit golden hair begins to dance in the wind. She walks to her life, to her freedom against the sea of green.

"Thank you for not asking my daughter to stay," her father says to me. "I'm very aware of the way she feels about you and that's why I made sure there's one seat for you in this helicopter. It will take us to safety, out of this war."

His words hit me so hard my consciousness dissociates from my body. I want nothing more than to get out of this hell with her. From the corner of my eye, I see Aleyna boarding the helicopter with her family, and a sense of peace washes over me like the Lebanese waterfall in the mountains.

Torn inside, I am deeply moved by this generous offer from someone I barely know. "I didn't come to Lebanon alone, sir. There are three of us Americans left here, and I couldn't live with myself abandoning my friends to die in this war."

He gazes at the castle he has built, takes a deep breath of the spicy, woody fragrance of the cedar trees that surround it, and he glimpses at the rising smoke in the distance.

Turning back to me with pain in his eyes, he looks into mine and his voice warms. "This is not America, this is Lebanon. Don't let your idealistic values get you killed here, Ashe. You're a good man, but a hard soul to save. Hope is scarce in the Middle East, but somehow I hope you survive this war, so one day I can call you *eb-nee*."

"Thank you, sir," I say, unsure of what he means.

With a firm handshake, he pulls me in and hugs me. As he walks steadfastly toward the helicopter, he signals to the pilot with his hand to lift off. Frozen in the vast green grass, I see the confusion on Aleyna's face slowly turning into despair and her screaming my name over the whoosh of the chopper's spinning blade. I will forever curse this day, forcing me to let go of her hand, but how can I not remain thankful for having the honor to hold it?

This moment pulls at me in opposite directions and tears my heart. Knowing that Aleyna is leaving toward safety is the only sanity I have to hold on to. Her father tucks his head down as he boards. The loudness grows and the power of the helicopter's wind blows the tears off my face.

My grandmother, Vincenta Mow, always told me that no prayer goes unanswered and so I pray, I beg God, if one of us can make it out of this hell, let it be Aleyna.

The helicopter lifts off the ground as her screams become inaudible, and then her silhouette disappears on the Mediterranean horizon.

THE FINGER OF FATE

"A blind eye that covered the sun."

Before I can close the door at the chalet, Danny and Anwar run over to hug me. Brothers, we stand arms crossed together, intertwined with each other's fate like a Celtic knot. It is obvious from the five o'clock shadows under their eyes that they had both been up most of the night, worrying and wondering if they'd see the morning.

I tell them about the choice that I faced and ask Danny what *eb-nee* means?

He looks at me with a certain pride. "'Son'... it means 'my son.'"

A humble smirk raises the corner of my sad lips.

Anwar untangles himself from our brotherly embrace and gives me an update. "Well, this is the situation. We haven't heard from Sana. The US Embassy abandoned us. Michelle called us an hour ago to let us know she made it out. Now you're telling us Aleyna's gone too. What the hell are we waiting for here, death? That's it. Let's make a move."

In a split-second moment of clarity, I think Beirut is only about 70 or so miles from Damascus, how hard could it be to get to the Syrian border if we set out before the nighttime bombing. Michelle did it alone.

Danny, looking at both of us with sorrowful eyes, says, "Sorry, guys. I feel responsible for bringing you into this mess. For once in our lives, I really wanted to do something incredible, to touch the stars. I can't sacrifice us anymore waiting here for Sana."

Touched by his words, I reach into my pocket and fish out the diamond ring, still in my jeans, proof of a life that slipped away from us all. "Beirut gave me a glimpse of what life could be, but war took it all away."

"It didn't take everything, Ashe. Not yet. Let's fight for what we have left," Danny replies and dangles the possibility of escape out of this violent chaos. Although the situation feels bleak, he always seems to have another ace up his sleeve. "Let's go. We need to hurry before the sun goes down."

It feels strange driving around a city under attack, windows open, stereo blasting Led Zeppelin. Racing through the deserted, mangled streets, some lanes are so damaged from the bombs that Danny has to drive on the opposite traffic lanes to keep us moving forward.

The road looks familiar despite the dusty daylight. "I think I've been here before," I say, trying to jolt my memory.

Danny clutches the steering wheel and drives faster. "This is our only chance to get out of Lebanon. Trust me, boys, this is going to work. I can feel it!"

I am cautiously optimistic as we careen through the curving streets up the hillside, until I recognize the side of the road where I relieved my bladder a few months back.

"Really? Marwan? That's your 'grand' plan, Danny? God help us!" I say, smacking my hand on the armrest.

"Who's Marwan?" Anwar asks with a nervous suspicion.

"Oh, you'll see," I reply sarcastically as we pull into the hidden house's security gate.

When Marwan buzzes us in, the shock on Anwar's face reminds me of my own after I first stepped into Marwan's "sanctuary."

"My friends, welcome! It's so nice to have visitors. A rare occurrence in these troubling times." Marwan hugs us as we introduce him to Anwar. He leads us to his spacious living room and the automatic doors close behind us.

Welcomed with hookah and tea in his luxurious, art-filled desert oasis, we almost forget the war raging outside.

Sitting down on the ornate pillows, looking at Marwan's face, I cannot reciprocate the smile he has in his eyes. I try to keep my cool, but all I can think is, this is a terrible mistake.

He picks up on my uneasiness and urge to get out of his secret arms lair. "My brother, Ashe, I see the war has opened your eyes so wide you now cannot unsee the truth. Living in Beirut during happy times is easy, but to stay during the dark times you learn the real reason of why we live like there's no tomorrow."

I gaze into his eyes as he takes a puff from his hookah, releasing a calming aroma into the air. "Tomorrow doesn't exist for me anymore, Marwan."

Taking a deep inhale, he leans over and pats me on my shoulder with a half-smile. "Well, now, my American friend, you are truly reborn as a Beiruti."

Danny slurps loudly as he finishes his tea. "*Habibi*, that's why we're here. I need to get my friends out of Lebanon. You are our last hope. Can you help us?"

Anwar and I look at Marwan in anticipation as he smiles and says, "Can I help you? Of course, I can help you. You should have come to me a long time ago. Now the Israeli army has tightened their grip and made Lebanon a prison. The sea, ground and air blockades have made all ways of getting out of Lebanon a no man's land."

"But you can help us?" Anwar repeats anxiously.

"Of course I can help you! I'm Marwan," he replies with almost comical boldness.

"I knew it! Thank you, God," Danny says, patting his own chest.

Seeing the hope light up in our eyes, Marwan proudly goes on, "But I only have three life vests, so you will have to choose which one of you goes without it. My boat is docked in the marina. It is one of the fastest boats in Lebanon. I will zoom you straight for Cyprus. There you can take a plane home. Easy—"

"Wait a minute!" Anwar interrupts him, irritated by his ridiculous propositions. "Didn't you just say there is an Israeli naval blockade? How are we going to get through it?"

"My friend, survival is just luck. Look, that is how I'm still alive."

All three of us stare at each other, realizing that the years of living as an arms dealer have taken a toll on his judgment. Dealing with warlords and mercenaries, he lives his life, bouncing like a ball on a roulette table.

"With all due respect, Marwan, and thank you for trying to help us, but after seeing what the Israeli submarine did to the naval base in Jounieh, a speedboat is not a chance I'm willing to take. In my humble opinion, we wouldn't last ten minutes," I tell him, realizing I may just die in this inferno.

Anwar looks deflated. "I agree with Ashe."

Every possibility of a way out seems to evaporate. Danny is calm but can't hide the disappointment in his eyes. "Do you have any other ideas, Marwan?"

"I have a small plane in Tripoli. I sometimes use it to get cargo to Africa, but it's not that fast. We would have to fly low to avoid getting detected," he says, letting us down further.

Anwar is quite incensed. "A small plane against an air blockade of Israeli fighter jets? Are you nuts?!"

We now are in full view of the mindset of an arms dealer who walks that thin fine line between life and death every day. Before hope abandons us once more, Marwan snaps his fingers loudly and says, "I have it! Let me make a call. Sit, sit." He motions for us to sit back down as he rushes to the corner of the room and gets out a small black briefcase from a hidden closet. He snaps it open and pulls out a satellite phone and dials a number. We sit quietly, looking at each other while Marwan speaks in a language I haven't yet heard in Lebanon.

"What's he saying?" I ask Danny.

"I don't know. I don't speak Russian," he replies, worried as his brown eyes grow bigger.

"Russian? Fuck me!" Anwar says, covering his face with both hands. "I have no words."

"Perfect, perfect, perfect. It's done! Marwan is going to get you out, my friends, as I promised," he says cheerily, putting his satellite phone back into the briefcase.

Danny and I look up intently while Anwar refuses to lift his head from the shield of his hands, shaking his head and repeating "fuck" over and over.

Marwan flops back down on the cushions. "In my line of business, favors are worth more than gold and for my childhood friend, I redeemed a big favor owed to me," he tells us with his world-weary demeanor. "There are two ex-KGB Russian spies living in Beirut. They have been hiding here for a long time. I can't tell you why they owe me, but they can get you out through Syria."

"This sounds the most doable, Marwan," Danny says, full of trust in his friend's ability. "I can't thank you enough."

"How can they get us out and when?" Anwar finally picks up his head, unconvinced.

"They said you'll have to travel through the night's cover to make it harder for the war jets to target you," Marwan explains the plan to us in the most serious tone he's ever used. "They'll be at your chalet at sundown, Danny, in two fast cars. Pack only what you absolutely need to take in order to keep their cars light. They will get you through the Hezbollah territory to the Syrian border, *Inshallah*, God willing. From there, they will take you through the Syrian desert to Amman, Jordan, where you can finally take a flight home, my friends."

"What about you, Marwan? Aren't you coming with us?" Danny asks, putting his arm around him.

"No, my friend, Marwan is at peace during war. No one can push me out of my home. If they come for me in this one, look, I show you..." He pauses mid-sentence and leads us to the kitchen. He pushes a hidden latch and moves the refrigerator to the side of the wall to reveal a hidden escape tunnel.

"Oh my gosh, it's so dark. Where does it go?" Anwar asks with wide-eyed intrigue.

"It goes down the mountain to my second house."

"That's amazing. Seems like you have it all figured out," I say, praising him.

He shoots me a seen-it-all-before fatalistic look. "I do, *habibi*! Okay, my friends, hurry now. You mustn't waste any time. Remember, pack light, have cash, trust no one and watch out for each other. And with God's blessing, you'll get out." He hugs us and hurries us out onto our journey.

Back at the chalet in my room, as I pack my clothes, I look around to determine which items to take. Nestled in a corner is my Egyptian papyrus, safely housed in a yellow hieroglyph-decorated roll-up tube. I grab it along with my bursting Louis Vuitton Keepall Bandoulière and saunter to the living room to make one last call.

"Hi, Pop. Is Mom home? Okay, put me on the speaker," I say to him as he confirms they are both home and I hear my mother's excited, disbelieving shouts in the background. "Thank you for your kind emails. Things are getting much worse over here. Every night, the casualty numbers rise. This country is in total shambles. I just wanted to tell you I love you. I've followed my heart here, and I have no regrets about the life I've led, so if something happens to me just know I'm at peace."

My mom screams at me down the phone, "Don't you do something stupid! Stay put. We wrote to our senator and congressional representative to get you guys out. My church is praying for you every Sunday. Steve, don't leave for the border, you'll die." I hear her crying before I have to hang up. She knows this is our last phone call.

Coming down the stairs, I see two older Mercedes-Benz sedans, one in a silvery gray and the other in a creamy beige. I laugh sarcastically inside, thinking I'm about to travel through a Hezbollah stronghold, driven by ex-KGB Russian spies, speeding in battered old cars from the 80s, as Israeli rockets rain down on us.

Can't make this shit up, Rodger.

I stride up to Danny and see a familiar face.

"Ashe, you remember Farid? He's coming with us," he says as if I'm supposed to know this and not be surprised by our uninvited guest.

"Yes, I remember. From the clubs in LA. I didn't know you were in Lebanon. Hopefully, we live to party again," I reply morbidly.

Farid gives me a quick handshake and half-hug. "So, Ashe, we're going to draw straws to see who goes by himself in the car with the luggage. We can't all fit and someone has to make sure these Russians don't drive away with our stuff." As he finishes, he holds out his hand with four white straws. It's already known that whoever draws the shortest straw is on his own.

While we stand looking at the four straws, I see Anwar shooting him a long, hard stare, annoyed. "Isn't that the least of our problems? Can't the Russians simply put bullets in our heads, dump our bodies in the middle of the mountains and take everything we have, anyway?"

"Shut up, Anwar. We don't have time for this shit. Let's draw," Danny replies, hurrying us up.

I reach out to Farid's outstretched hand and cover the straws with my palm. I look Danny and Anwar dead in the eyes and tell them, "I'm not drawing against my brothers. I'll go alone with the Russian and our luggage."

With a sigh of relief, they all agree. The Russians urge us to stop pissing about and hurry to their cars. "We go now," one of them yells.

We pay the Russians in cash, 200 American dollars each. That's how much our lives are now worth. While they are packing our bags into the car, I take a minute and walk alone to the shoreline to see my last Lebanese scarlet sunset. It reflects in the windows of the buildings against the cedar mountains as the full moon rises above. After a silent prayer, I take out my camera and snap a photo before my Russian honks impatiently for me to get in.

Sliding into the passenger seat beside him, I buckle my seatbelt tightly and notice our stacked luggage in the backseat. As we race away through the desert streets with the sunset to our backs, I see the shadows of my friends' heads in the Mercedes in front of us. Making an abrupt turn onto the highway, I get a good glimpse of my driver, who looks a proper Glasnost gangster with his pale glacial-green eyes and cold manner. Immediately, I get the sense he has killed many men in his line of work. The wrinkles on his face show a soul who has lived in an immense internal torment. He looks to be in his early 50s, balding and gripping the steering wheel tight with his big worn hands.

The car stinks of stale tobacco. I notice the ashtray overflowing with cigarette butts. Sitting in silence, too scared to start a conversation with him, I find some comfort in the engine's humming. Snaking through the side roads, we chase the other Mercedes into the nightfall at a dizzying 100 mph or more. My heart beats faster as our headlights are barely keeping up with the rear of their car. Then the Russian does the most audacious thing I could imagine and turns off the headlights, pulling down the windows. Weaving along the curving mountains in his clapped-out Mercedes at an insane speed, I can no longer see the road nor the brake lights of my friends ahead of us.

Gripping the door handle as I get flung around like a marionette with each sharp turn and hairpin bend, I finally say in frustration, "Why did you turn off the lights?"

He glances at me, frowning, and leans into the steering wheel without a word, trying to keep his eye on the road and the sky.

"Can you please turn on the lights and slow down," I ask him again, but he remains silent as he pushes the gas pedal to the floor. It is at this moment I realize he doesn't speak any English. *At all!* My fright and anger are indistinguishable. A thought simmers in me that my friends know I can't speak Arabic or Russian, yet here I am without a means of communication with my driver.

I take a deep breath, but before I can lash out, the Russian points to his ear with his finger. He wants me to listen to the night, he wants me to hear something in the white fog. I close my eyes, holding tight to the car, and I can hear the other Mercedes' wheels screeching on the turns of the road. I guess my Russian knows what he's doing, and I should just shut the fuck up before I disturb his concentration and we end up at the bottom of this mountain.

Minutes turn into hours before the white fog lifts and we come upon a ghost town on the other side of the mountain. Going through the deserted backroads in darkness is the safest, if circuitous, way of reaching the Syrian border. At the crossroad, my driver hesitates to turn but ultimately goes left. His face changes, becomes unsure as he drives slower through the abandoned town and looks around with a frown between his big, hairy brows.

"We're lost? Aren't we? Why do I even bother saying anything? You don't understand a word I'm saying, do you?" I say to him, frustrated.

He looks at me with his glacial-green scowl before we hear his phone ringing. He picks it up immediately and starts speaking in Russian.

"Is that Danny? Danny's car? Danny! Danny! I need to talk to you," I yell frantically beside him.

Making a U-turn, he hands me his Motorola cellphone.

"Danny? This guy doesn't speak any English, and he got us lost," I yell into the phone.

"Hey, *habibi*. You're not lost. He just made a wrong turn. We pulled over and are waiting for you. You're like a minute behind us."

"This guy is out of his mind. He races without headlights on," I continue venting to Danny.

"That's why you're still alive. It's harder for fighter jets to target you speeding with no lights through the night. He knows what he's doing. You have to trust him," he tells me confidently before the Russian snatches the phone from me, putting it on the side of his seat.

I look up and notice Danny's car right in front of us as we speed up again. Relieved at the sight, my eyes wander through the surrounding landscape. I see immense mansions, dark and empty, some with interior lights still on, with gates and front doors wide open. What in the world would cause these prosperous people to abandon their gorgeous homes? We are so far away from the war here. As I ponder all of this, in shock, the sky lights up white above our car, and with a thundering jolt, a rocket flies over us, high into the night sky.

"Hezbollah," the Russian says, glancing at me and pointing his big, worn finger into the sky. Now I know why the mansions are deserted and why we're racing for our lives. I've never been so deathly frightened. I don't want to die in this car next to a stranger in a foreign land.

The phone rings again and the Russian picks up. This time I can hear a woman's voice shouting on the other end. He retorts back at her when suddenly I overhear a high-pitched little girl's voice. His brow relaxes and his shoulders drop. He mumbles his words gently as the little girl's voice lightens up his wrinkled face. He hangs up and puts the phone on the side of his leather seat again. I realize in this moment that he, too, is risking his life to save mine, an American. My jaded westernized view of *evil* Russians crumbles. I finally see the reformed gentle bear next to me, and feel I can trust him now with my life. Still, I couldn't help wondering what kind of favor he owed Marwan? Clearly, $200 is not something that would rip this man away from his family during these terrifying times of war.

The car rattles at this breakneck speed as we pass an abandoned gas station on the right. Through the dusty passenger window, I see six armed men wearing black turbans, sitting on ammunition boxes, chilling, smoking their hookah, with their RPGs resting against their makeshift chairs. Without a reaction, they look at us racing by them. My face goes numb.

The Russian chuckles and shrugs his broad shoulders, saying, "Hezbollah."

I guess they must be on a cigarette break, Rodger.

Looking down the dusty road, I see an abandoned car with its lights still on. Then another with its doors still open, then another and then hundreds, a sight fit for a dark apocalyptic movie set. Incredibly, we've made it to the Lebanese-Syrian border. Already stopped ahead of us, I see my friends waiting for me beside their car.

My Russian driver heaves a deep sigh of relief. I rush out of the car toward my friends and get a hug from Danny and Anwar. We walk into the Lebanese-Syrian border checkpoint, which surprisingly is empty at this time of the night.

When we enter the checkpoint, the guards look at us with disbelief, as if we are ghosts. I assume very few make it here alive now. The guards eerily stamp our passports and escort us to the Syrian side. As the Lebanese border gates open, the Syrian border security force dressed in fatigues greets us. I see hundreds of Lebanese refugees in line, some sleeping on the ground, dirty and pitiful, waiting to be granted passage to safety.

"Man, this line is going to take weeks," Anwar says, disappointed.

Danny waves at the Russians, who have already passed the border with their Russian passports and are parked waiting for us.

Farid comes running toward us. "This way, come," he says in a breathless rush. "This insane line is for Lebanese citizens only."

We follow him inside the Syrian border station and see a tiny handwritten sign on a sheet of white paper that says: *US passports only*.

There is no one in this line. We walk straight to the front while I catch glimpses of the desperate expressions of the people waiting in the other line. In some deranged way, it reminds me of when Ricky would wave me through the velvet ropes of the Hollywood clubs, where lines would stretch for blocks. But there is no Ricky here and we are not in yet. Instead, there is a young Syrian soldier who glares at us with disdain.

The soldier asks us for our passports and looks over them carefully, holding our pictures to our faces for comparison. He stamps my passport and says, "Stevens, go."

He stamps Anwar's passport and motions with his hand to pass the gate to join me, then says, "Farbish, go."

He stamps Farid's passport and says, "Gomez, go."

When we hear the name, Anwar smirks and whispers to me, "Who the fuck is Gomez?! Whose passport did he steal?"

I stand frozen without a word next to Anwar as Farid slowly walks toward us.

As the Syrian soldier is reviewing Danny's passport, Anwar grabs Farid's passport and glares at it, "Who the fuck is Kamron Gomez? Are you trying to get us killed?"

Farid shoots Anwar a cold glare to shut up as we're drawing the attention of the other guards at the station.

The checkpoint guard stares at Danny's passport, then at Danny, and hands it back and waves him off to go back to Lebanon. Our mouths drop. We walk back to the soldier and Anwar and Farid try to explain to him that Danny is our friend and an American citizen, but our words fall on deaf ears. In a desperate attempt, we pool a thousand dollars between us, put the cash in Danny's passport and hand it to the soldier. He gives us an icy look and walks away into the back of the station with our money and Danny's passport. The several minutes that the Syrian soldier is gone drag like hours. Finally, he comes back, followed by an older, higher-ranked soldier.

"Oh shit, he's a general," Danny whispers to me. "I don't understand why they're not letting me in."

The general walks up to us, the multiple medals adorned on his uniform, sparkling in the yellow lamp light.

"Danny Bitar," he says in a deep voice, pointing his finger to the smoke-filled Lebanese skies, "you are not American. You are a Bitar, a son of a Lebanese general. You are Lebanese. Go back to your country and await your fate."

FIELDS OF GREEN LIGHTS

"There is more God inside you than in any book."

The old general's calloused finger hangs in the air in front of our eyes. He didn't fire a gunshot, but with his finger and a blind eye, his words become Danny's death sentence. The Lebanese refugees in the other line gasp in horror as our story unfolds. The general hands Danny his passport with the cash still inside before retreating back into his office. There's nothing else we can do. As we walk Danny back to the crossing, I notice my Russian driver getting onto the Lebanese side and unloading our luggage. He's getting ready to take Danny back to Jounieh.

"Danny, I'm coming with you," I say hopelessly as I see my Egyptian papyrus resting with my LV bag on the sandy ground next to the other car.

"No, *habibi*. You've turned down your life before for our friendship. Don't make the same mistake twice. I'll be fine. This is my country. I'll figure something out. You go, there's nothing left in Lebanon for you now. Get the hell out of here," he replies, giving me a long hug and pushing me toward the border gate.

With tears in my eyes, I grab my LV bag and the papyrus and walk to the gate. Turning around to take my last glimpse of Danny before getting into the car, unbelievably, I see him pull down his pants and stick his ass out, giving the middle finger to the shocked faces of the Syrian border patrol. The hundreds of Lebanese refugees in the line erupt in laughter, followed by clapping and cheerful howls.

Danny waves at me one last time and, with a big smile, disappears inside the Mercedes.

Driving into the darkness of the night, I see a sign in our headlights that reads: *Our dear guests, you are welcomed to ASSAD'S SYRIA, in case of any complaints, or any comments, regarding your comfortable entry to SYRIA, please send a direct fax to the office of the General Customs Director.*

Your comfort is our concern.

We wish you a good stay in hospitable SYRIA.

Welcome to SYRIA.

We can't stop laughing at this hilariously ironic sign. And for a few moments, it's just the distraction we need in all this bleakness.

I am stuffed into the backseat next to the right window with my bag and papyrus on my lap. The front passenger seat is filled with luggage. Anwar and Farid are crammed beside me, with bags on their laps to accommodate the lack of space from losing the other Mercedes, which had to go back to Lebanon with Danny.

Anwar breaks the silence. "It's a crime against humanity what the Syrians just did to Danny. I hope that's not the last time we see him. I pray Danny and your comrade get home safe."

The Russian, who is a tall, thin man in his 50s with silver-flecked sandy-brown hair, blue eyes and pale skin, stares at the dark road in silence for a minute, as if he is collecting the appropriate words, and hisses under his breath, "Americans."

I'm shocked to learn this ex-KGB spy speaks English. Just my luck. I had to be in the car with the one who didn't.

The Russian's eyes briefly beam at Anwar through the rearview mirror as he says, "Whose bombs do you think Israel is using to kill Lebanese children?"

I get chills as his words reach deep into my heart, remembering the dead little girl pulled out of the rubble and her parents screaming in despair. Innocent lives taken by the mindless war with American taxpayer-funded weapons. I nudge Anwar to shut up as he opens his mouth to reply to the Russian with something snarky. The last thing we want to do is cross our surly Russian comrade.

Anwar sees the sadness on my face and leans back without a word. I notice Farid with his head resting against the headrest, asleep with his mouth open. I look out the window onto the dark road. A patch of lonely desert bush catches my eye against the mountains and reminds me of the road to Marwan's house. I'm wondering if Marwan's good deed of saving a few lives tonight will be accounted for against the weight of death his business brought to the world. There's a story in the Bible that always fascinated me. After Judas Iscariot betrays Jesus for 30 silver coins, he comes to the realization of what he has done. In desperate remorse, he attempts to return the silver coins to the Pharisee priests before he hangs himself. The priests refuse to take their money back for themselves, as it is now stained with the blood of the innocent. They decide to use Judas's cursed coins and turn their evil deed into a righteous one by purchasing Akeldama, a potter's field, as a burial site for the unknown, unclaimed or indigent. I wonder if Marwan, the merchant of death, purchased his potter's field with our three lives.

In the nighttime gloom, I'm blinded by the headlights of a car speeding toward us. Our Russian slams on the brakes, jolting Farid awake.

Anwar shoots him a sideways glance. "Why are we stopping?"

"Wait here," the Russian says hastily, getting out of the car. His slim body slowly moves to the hood of our car, and as he waits, a shadowy figure emerges from behind the headlights of the car stopped in front of us.

Farid, just woken up and wide-eyed, goes into a blind panic. "Oh shit! They're going to kill us! Anwar, get into the driver's seat! We've gotta get out of here. Let's go!"

"What the fuck's wrong with you? Go where? We're in the middle of the desert. This isn't a dream. Wake up," Anwar snaps, irked as I sit there paralyzed, straining to hear what the two men in the headlights are saying.

Suddenly, the Russian walks to the left passenger door and opens it swiftly, saying to Farid, "Get out and come dig your graves! We bury your asses here."

We all look at each other in horror and Farid stumbles out of the car, visibly trembling.

The Russian bursts out laughing and slaps Farid on the back. "Relax, I kid with you. You don't like Russian joke, no? I'm not allowed in Jordan. This is Roman, he will get you to Amman."

We all nervously exhale but can't bring ourselves to laugh as we gather our belongings. Walking on the sandy road to the other car, I overhear the Russian mumble, rolling his eyes and throwing his hands in the air, "Americans."

The new car is much smaller and older. I can't see the make in the dark, but it's one of those boxy, tinny old cars with rusty, chipped paint. Roman tidies the luggage into the trunk and string ties the ajar trunk door to the bumper. Even though the car is smaller, this allows us to have more room inside to sit comfortably on the old, frayed leather seats with areas of exposed yellow foam cushion.

The dull light from our car's headlights gives me the feeling that we are descending farther into darkness. I'm tired as hell, but I'm too scared to close my eyes. Resting my forehead on the dirty window, I whisper a prayer for Danny to get home safely. As I'm praying, we drive over a desert mound, and I see fields of little green lights, high in the night sky. A city of green Christmas lights flickering in the distance. Driving closer, I notice nothing else but the green lights. My ignorance compels me to ask our silent driver, "What are these green lights?"

Roman looks at me in the rearview mirror and says, "Those, my friend, are minarets. The towers of the mosques. Green is symbolic of paradise in Islam. You see, it's sad that you won't find any mall, theater or club here. This is an example of how to breed strict religious fanatics."

I look out the window, captivated by the green lights in the desert. "Well, maybe their religion is all they want."

Roman smirks at me and continues driving without another word.

I rest my head back on the dusty window. My eyelids get heavy, hypnotized by the green lights, so I close my tired eyes.

Several hours later the car stops suddenly and my body shoves forward as I'm awakened.

"We're here!" Roman yells, getting out of the car and untying the string to free our luggage from the grip of his small trunk.

In the inky-purple predawn light, I look out the window and I see a green sign for Amman Airport in front of us.

"Thank God, we made it," Farid says, excited, leaping out to stretch and grab his bag.

"Anwar, Anwar, we're here!" I shake him out of his nap.

"We're almost home, brother. Now we just have to get out of here," Anwar replies, his voice still groggy with sleep. "This is a dangerous country right now for Americans. We don't want to get kidnapped here. This is where they take you, demand a ransom from your family and send little pieces of you in a box before they behead you. I'm so happy we're leaving."

"Good to know." I try not to make eye contact with anyone as we pass a multitude of people. It looks like a refugee camp. People everywhere, sleeping on their bags on the floor, the blistering sun reflecting off their sweaty skin.

Jordan is the size of Portugal, a peaceful desert oasis surrounded by Syria, Israel, Iraq and Saudi Arabia, the world's biggest political hotspot. It doesn't have the culture of crazed radicalism of its troublesome neighbors, but it still feels like a dangerous and unstable place.

Farid leads us to the departures side of the airport. Walking inside the light gray-stone terminal, the thick stench of body odor smacks us in the face. Inside, there are even more people hoping to leave here. Farid walks up to the Middle East Airlines gate check-in officer.

"All three of us have MEA tickets out of Lebanon," he explains, "but their airport was bombed, so we need the next flight to Los Angeles. Thanks!"

The airline check-in officer laughs, motioning at the crowds of people squatting at the airport, but goes through the motions on his computer.

"We have no empty seats out of Jordan for the next two weeks," he says, smiling, a hint of malice in his voice. He hands back our passports and tickets to our petrified faces. We cannot move from the weight of how bad our situation just became.

This pushes Anwar to the edge. "We're fucked," he mutters.

The check-in officer sees the terror in our eyes, and as he turns toward another customer, he says quietly, not knowing we can hear, "Stupid Americans."

JORDAN'S SUPERMAN

"I am a silent mustard seed in the old desert."

O ur naive excitement of going home only intensifies the disappointment in our walk of shame heading out of the airport.

Anwar is still freaking out. "We're so fucked. We should've stayed in Lebanon," he says quietly to us. "I'd rather take my chances with an Israeli bomb than have my body being dismembered by Al-Qaeda for ransom. We went from bad to worse."

Before we get to the automatic door exit, Farid grabs my shoulder, pulls me closer and whispers intensely, "Ashe, the minute we walk out these doors, we are prey. The only thing we have going for us is that you also look Middle Eastern. Anwar and I speak Arabic but you don't, so as long as you don't open your mouth once, we should be okay. You must blend in, brother. Just remember, if anyone finds out that you're an American, we all die here. You understand?"

The weight of the moment with the intense heat rushing in through the double doors sends me into a mirage of Rodger yelling at me in mask class: *"Do not speak or cry! Listen!"*

I got it, Rodger.

I look at Farid's eyes and Anwar's concerned face and nod in agreement. We walk out into the stifling desert air to grab a taxi back to downtown Amman. Farid walks up to a payphone to make a call.

The taxi pulls in and we load our luggage. Farid comes back with a plan. "We'll be staying at the Grand Hyatt Amman for the next couple of weeks." Apparently, Farid, the international playboy, has a girlfriend even in Jordan, and she conveniently works at the booked-solid hotel and was able to get us a room.

"We should be safe there," he tells us, adding as an afterthought, "But after the three hotel Al-Qaeda suicide bombings last year, I guess nowhere in this land is safe for Americans."

Our hotel room is much smaller than what we are used to back in America. Only a couple feet away from the entrance is one king-size bed and a small glass table, resting up against the window with two chairs on each side. The view is of Amman's overpopulated concrete jungle with a sprinkle of vegetation. The dense monotone-beige architecture gives me a claustrophobic feeling.

Before getting comfortable, we dial Danny's number and

are thankful to learn that he is fine and made it back to his chalet. I also call Aleyna, but her phone rings without an answer. I shut the curtains and enjoy a long, hot shower, washing away the desert heat and sand. When I come out of the bathroom, I see Farid and Anwar already collapsed, fast asleep on the king-size bed, still in their shoes. We are all beyond exhausted. I take a seat on the green armchair next to the table and put my feet up on the other chair. The humming of the air conditioner lulls me into a deep sleep. I have forgotten what it feels like to rest without worrying if I will wake up.

The next morning, the sliding of an envelope under the door startles all of us awake. Anwar leaps out of bed to pick it up and opens it as I pull the curtains open, unsure of what time of day it is.

"You gotta be kidding me," Anwar says, looking at the beige sheet of paper as the morning light illuminates his face.

Glancing at the digital alarm clock next to the bed, I realize we've been asleep for 18 hours.

I rush over to read the letter, and after seeing the amount on what appears to be our hotel bill, I ask, "Is this for the whole two weeks?"

"Lemme see!" Farid says, ripping the bill out of my hands, his face quickly turning pale. "What the hell? $568 for one night?"

Anwar walks up to the window and opens the curtains wider, gazing out at the sea of crumbling beige buildings and ugliness. "Yup, this is not Vegas. Not by a long shot. Six hundred dollars for this shithole? Give us a break. We're refugees, for fuck's sake!"

"Let me take care of this, I got this," Farid says, picking up the phone and calling his "girlfriend."

Anwar and I sit at the edge of the bed, listening to Farid yelling into the phone in Arabic.

I elbow Anwar. "What's he saying?"

"We're screwed, that's what he's saying," Anwar says, rolling his eyes and shaking his head.

"Whaddya mean? What happened?" I ask, suddenly worried, as Farid's voice rises.

"The *girlfriend* just found out that this piece of shit slept with her cousins," Anwar says, slightly vexed.

"Wait, wait... *cousins*? As in plural, with an *s*?" I ask, stunned.

"Yeah! Unbelievable. Just our luck."

Farid finally gets off the phone and the room goes silent again.

"Obviously, we can't afford to stay here for two weeks," he says calmly, shrugging his shoulders.

Anwar just glares at him in fury.

"What? Don't look at me like that. Who could've predicted that a war would break out after her cousins and I had some fun on a friend's yacht."

I stood up between them to referee. "We can't undo the past, but how are we going to solve this problem now. This is a big fucking mess we're in."

"Well, we're not that fucked. She said there's a rental apartment building literally across the street," Farid says, pointing to the dilapidated grey building on the corner. "We can go there and try our luck to see if there's a vacancy. It's sketchy and not as nice, but we don't really have the budget for any other option."

We split the outrageous bill and head out with our luggage onto the hellishly hot sidewalk. Amman is known as the "white city" because much of it is built from limestone. The light-colored buildings outside against the rays of the scorching desert sun are almost blinding to my tired eyes.

Walking up to the apartment building, Farid motions at me to wait outside with Anwar while he negotiates for a room. He comes back a few minutes later with a green tagged key. Our room is the first on the right after passing the bell desk. The skinny, bearded young attendant gives me an ominous look as we sweep past.

The room is simple and stuffy, with a taint odor, and looks like it's never been cleaned. With one large, hard bed, an old wooden desk, a dusty fan and rusting metal bars on the outside of the windows, it feels like a prison.

Without talking to each other, we put our luggage away in the small closet, and Anwar signals with his hand lifting to his open mouth for us to leave to get something to eat.

Walking out the door, I feel the front-desk guy's eyes searing right through me. Maybe I'm paranoid, but I may as well have *American* stamped on my forehead with a bullseye.

Driving through the streets of Amman, squeezed together in a clapped-out old taxi, I see crowds of people walking on the streets. It somehow reminds me of an ancient version of New York City, but in Jordan, all the women are wearing hijabs and most are in burkas. At a stoplight on the right-hand side of the street, I notice a small mosque with its front doors wide open, where a cleric is giving out food on paper plates to the homeless children of the city.

The sight of this cleric encircled by these little, wide-eyed children reminds me of Aleyna when she first arrived at the school with her gifts. It reverberates inside of me, a blissful time that seems so, so far away now, as I silently smile.

We arrive at one of the nicest McDonald's I've ever seen. As we are eating in complete silence, I get an ill-omened feeling, noticing that we're the only ones dining here. I think I'm being paranoid, but the staff from behind the counter keeps looking at us intensely.

I look at Anwar, who nervously stops eating mid-bite, gets up and motions for us to finish and leave. Scurrying outside, I notice a rusting white van with blacked-out windows. Anwar sees it coming toward us, picking up his pace, and tries frantically to hail a taxi. With all of our arms waving in the air now, I glimpse the white van's door swiftly sliding open.

"Get in! Get in!" Anwar shouts, shoving me into a taxi.

Within seconds I find myself in the backseat, squeezed in between my friends, who are both shouting at the driver in Arabic. The driver speeds up manically like Amira and my neck whiplash-es. Glancing out the rear window, I see three men running back into the white van with only their eyes peeking through their shemagh scarves.

While Farid is yelling at the driver in Arabic, Anwar leans over and whispers, "I saw these guys waiting for us outside. You know who eats at a McDonald's in Jordan? Stupid Americans."

I look behind again and see the white van catching up to us before I get thrown to the side from a swift turn. Farid continues to scream at the driver, who looks flustered and is yelling back with what sounds like a question mark in his voice.

Suddenly, we come to a complete stop and the driver furiously is trying to get rid of us, waving us out of his taxi.

Anwar whispers to me again, "He wants us out. But we're dead if he doesn't start moving."

With Farid still arguing with the driver, I see the white van flying around the corner and charging straight toward us. Through the rear window, I notice a billboard down the street advertising the lost city of Petra. Grabbing Anwar back inside the taxi, I shout in my best Middle Eastern accent that I can possibly muster, "Petra!"

"Petra?" the driver repeats.

Farid and Anwar look at each other and respond to the driver in Arabic, waving money in his face. He accelerates as the white van is just a couple cars behind us.

Weaving between cars, I feel my stomach clench in fear of being caught. Imagining myself as a jihadi hostage, I think this is the end, there's no way we'll get out of here alive. The adrenaline is unbelievable.

Heading onto the highway and farther from the city, the Jihadists are still tailing us, until, nearly an hour into our journey, the white van turns back through the barren desert road.

Watching the van making a screeching U-turn, our taxi driver smiles and says to our surprise in broken English, "Allah smiles upon you today, my friends. You tell me you in danger, I keep driving. In my religion we help, not kill. You safe with me. My name is Yusef."

Too scared to open my mouth, I look at Anwar as he leans across the front seat and says something in Arabic to Yusef.

"Yes, my English very good. They want your American friend in the middle," Yusef says, staring at me in the rearview mirror as we speed on the ancient King's Highway, the main artery of Jordan, what looks like a broad and endless desert road, surrounded by sparse rocky mountains and snaking through deep ravines and canyons.

Farid looks at the driver. "How did you know he's an American?"

Yusef chuckles and replies, "Look at him. The tattoos, he dress something different. He don't belong here."

Yusef's blunt honesty makes me laugh. "I take that as a compliment. But seriously, thank you for saving our lives, Yusef."

He turns around for a second to look at me and smiles, holding on to his weathered steering wheel with both hands.

Driving for a couple hours, we see nothing but uninhab-itable desert, long stretches of red sandstone cliffs towering over desolate terrain of red sand and rock outcroppings, without another living soul around, aside from a few birds of prey, ravens and desert larks, soaring across the skies. My eyes stumble upon a large tent, rising from the burnt-orange sand like a speckle in the sun. I'm spellbound by the elaborate design of the flowing tent and ask Yusef if he can pull over so I can take a picture.

"No, my friend, those the Bedouin. We must respect their space," Yusef explains. "They are nomadic people of this land. Their tribe travels the Wadi Rum desert and many others, their whole lives. Bedouin live in the old world, no one disturbs them."

Enchanted by the colorful fabrics and patterns of the fairly large rugs wrapping around the domed, sandy roof of the sizable tent, I start to wonder how free I really am. Drifting in the desert wind, right before me, inside of that magical tent are human beings who possess the quintessential definition of freedom. Their tent opens my eyes to the realization that I'm far from being an awakened nomad. Stuck in the world of greed and war, the nomad I thought I was is lost. Without a word, the Bedouins scream into my heart that this is the price you must pay for *un alma libre*. I bury my old eyes in the Jordanian desert as the faint sapphire moon in the distance lights my new path.

The passage to the lost city of Petra starts with the Siq, a long hike through the tall, narrow, curving red canyons. Pleased that he got us here safely, Yusef waits by his taxi to drive us back to Amman.

The facade of the treasury, Al-Khazneh, is embedded in a towering red mountain under the blazing blue sky. Gazing at the magnificence of this ancient archeological site, one of the world's wonders, which is awe-inspiring, surprisingly doesn't fill my vessel as much as the Bedouins' tent.

Wandering around the Rose City, once the prosperous capital of the Nabataean Arabs, a thought brews in my mind that freedom comes from within. It's not a place or a person, but a state of mind. The closest I ever got to that feeling was with Aleyna, living in the moment in Beirut. Leaving Petra's red stone waves toward Yusef's taxi, I come across a vendor selling an assortment of pirate copy DVDs, neatly laid out on a rug on the sandy ground. Noticing with excitement the *Superman* movie, which is currently showing in theaters in Hollywood, I buy it with glee.

Driving back to Amman, as the sun is diving into the orange Valley of the Moon, I look for the Bedouins' tent, but it seems to have vanished. But knowing it's somewhere out there, in the dusk, fills my vessel with a new interpretation of what a free life could be.

Enlivened inside, with the *Superman* DVD in hand, we walk into our dark room. Farid gets the first turn to use the shower. Even though it's almost early morning, I ask Anwar for his Mac so we can watch *Superman* together. We set his laptop on the bed on top of my bag. Resting our backs against the white chipped wall, we start the movie. It's one of those pirate copies, the worst quality you can imagine, recorded over someone's shoulder in a cinema, but we don't care. Superman gives us the strength to continue fighting so we can get back home to America.

Suddenly the bathroom door flings open, with the shower still running, and Farid, in a tiny towel, runs over dripping wet and slams Anwar's laptop shut.

"Are you fucking idiots?" he hisses at us through gritted teeth. "Are you trying to get us killed?"

Anwar looks at him perplexed and says quietly, "Bro, what the fuck is your problem?"

Farid tightens the towel around his waist and glares at us. "You have an American movie in English blasting on full volume in an apartment building where I was told tourists have gone missing!"

I look at him in shock. "Well, that's a piece of information you should've shared with us before coming here. Don't you think?"

He looks at me, flustered, realizing his mistake and his lack of transparency. As Farid opens his mouth to reply, we hear a weight move off our room's door. A shadow in a crack at the bottom of the door gets smaller and we hear quick footsteps fade away.

I get this sinister feeling that it's the bearded front-desk clerk. "Now they're creeping around our room spying on us," I say to my frightened friends. "That's it. We're dead."

MYSTIC SATELLITES OF MEMORY

"The winds of heaven blow for the people of the cedars."

For several seconds, before we can gather our thoughts, the running shower splashing against tiles is the only sound we hear. Holed up in our dingy apartment in the middle of nowhere, Anwar and I weigh our options whether to crash for a few hours or flee.

Anwar looks at me with fear in his eyes. "This room is going to be the last thing we will ever see if we don't leave right now."

Without another word, Farid emerges out of the bathroom, throws on his clothes, shoves his belongings into his bag, and Anwar and I pack up too. Within minutes, we're heading out the door. Anwar and I rush past the young bearded attendant.

In shock, he stops mid-word on the phone, seeing us check out in a hurry this early in the morning, days before our original departure time. In defiance, Farid hurls our green-tagged room key onto the attendant's desk. Then he darts out to the street, where Anwar and I are already loading a taxi. As our driver speeds away, I notice the attendant leaning over his desk to leer at us, frantically yelling on the phone.

At the Amman Airport, while taking out our luggage from the taxi's trunk, Anwar whispers in my ear, "Shit, man, that was close. That's the second time we almost got kidnapped. This is life or death now. We need to get the fuck outta here, ASAP."

Walking among the tsunami of refugees stranded at the airport because of the war in Lebanon, I realize my Levi's need to be pulled up every few steps. I've lost so much weight that I tighten my belt another notch, so I can keep up with my friends without losing my jeans.

Before reaching the MEA terminal, Farid motions with his hands for us to stop. "Let's sit here and plan this out," he tells us. "We need to find 'the guy.' The one person in charge who has the authority to bypass all the rules and get us on a plane out of here today. Look at how many people are desperately trying to leave. It's going to cost us a lot. How much do you guys have left?"

Anwar reaches into his pocket and fishes out a wad of US greenbacks. "I have almost a thousand here. How much do you have, Farid?"

Farid looks into his wallet and pulls out all the cash. "About the same. What about you, Ashe?"

I take out all the money and say in an uneasy tone. "Not a lot, only about 200 bucks."

My friends' heads slump down as Farid sighs and says, "That's not going to do it, brother. We don't have enough for all three of us."

Hopeless, I stare out of the airport windows thinking to myself, *I'll never leave this desert alive.* Suddenly, catching the reflection of a woman with long blond hair, I immediately think it's Aleyna. I spin around and sadly realize it was just a woman with a beige hijab teasing my imagination. I haven't eaten in days. I'm hungry, thirsty and have a headache from dehydration, so my mind is playing tricks on me in this ancient land. Looking at my friends' dejected faces, I catch my hand deep in my right pocket, subconsciously playing with a tiny object.

"Wait," I mumble.

Anwar and Farid stare at me when I reveal Aleyna's diamond-platinum engagement ring.

"Add this. It should be more than enough now."

Anwar puts his hand on my right shoulder, looking at the ring sparkling in the sun. "Man, are you sure?"

"It's just a ring, Anwar. In the end, love will save us all." I hand Farid the diamond.

Farid collects all of our cash and the ring and puts it together with our passports as we hunt with our eyes for "the guy" who looks easily bribable.

Three hours go by before we have a pretty good idea of who "the guy" is. When an opportunity presents itself that our guy is finally alone on a computer, Farid seizes the chance and nervously walks up to him.

From across the hallway, we watch Farid anxiously handing the guy our passports and valuables. The guy cautiously looks side to side and then types on the computer in front of him.

After about 15 minutes, Farid comes back, walking toward us with a muted smile. "I hope these tickets work because he took everything."

Anwar grabs the bundle of papers from his hand, looks for the ticket with his name on it. "Wait, there's a big problem here. These tickets have three different destinations."

"Yeah, I know. He could only get us on separate flights out of Jordan. The bigger problem is Ashe's flight leaves hours after ours."

Anwar looks at me with concern. "You need to go back, man, and make him change these tickets," he says to Farid with his hands in the air. "We can't leave Ashe alone here with no cash and for hours. Did you forget he doesn't speak any Arabic? What if the ticket he has is no good and he can't get home?"

Farid stares at our guy busy checking in travelers, momentarily considering the situation, then back at me. "I'm sorry, Ashe, but there's nothing I can do. It's what it is. My flight to Dubai is boarding in 15 minutes and Anwar's leaves in 30 minutes, flying to Hamburg, then to Los Angeles. You'll have to last here for six hours alone before your flight through Paris to LA, bud. If anything happens and you aren't allowed to board, just stay at the airport and call the US Embassy. Don't go back to the apartment, okay?"

I look at Farid, lift his bag off the floor and hand it to him. "Safe travels, my friend. Till next time."

He gives each of us a hug with one arm and sprints over to his gate without looking back. As we watch our friend disappear in the crowd, Anwar says, "I'm going to have to leave soon. I'm not good at goodbyes. Good luck, brother. Hopefully, I'll see you soon in LA."

He taps me on the shoulder and excitedly walks over toward his departure gate.

After both of my friends vanish within the bustle of this busy, heaving airport, I slump down on the floor. Leaning against the wall, I look up at the departures screen, and watch, one by one, their flights leaving Jordan. For the first time I'm truly alone, finding myself surrendered to the acceptance of my fate. Sitting here, I laugh to myself at all the plans I had in my life when suddenly I notice a small shadow hovering over me.

"Ciao!" A beautiful, amber-eyed, ten-year-old girl with golden-brown curls and high cheekbones smiles and hands me a small purple desert flower. I take it as a good omen.

"Hello. Thank you." Tears pool in my eyes through my smile. It's the first time a stranger has been kind to me in a very long time.

"Lucrezia! Lucrezia! *Vieni qui!*" I hear the little girl's mom calling her to the gate in front of us, where a flight to Rome is boarding.

"Don't be sad. I go now. Ciao!" She smiles and gallops to her parents.

"Ciao, Lucrezia!"

Hours go by and the moment of truth culminates as I hear overhead the boarding announcement for my flight to Paris.

The mix of hesitancy and excitement propels me toward the gate. Handing the flight attendant my ticket and passport, I hold my breath in anticipation. I let out a silent sigh when she hands me back my passport and ticket, waving me on board.

Still in disbelief that I'm actually heading home, with my head down, I slowly walk to my window seat. Frightened that this is all just a dream, I dare not show my emotions walking to the back of the plane. In my assigned seat, I clutch my arms around my Egyptian papyrus and rest my head against the window. As the packed plane lifts off from the runway, the passengers erupt with a uniform clap and cheer, relieved to be out of the old desert.

After a short while, looking out the window, I spot, glistening in the sun, the golden Dome of the Rock in Jerusalem. As we fly over Israel, I see no fires or smoke, no ruined buildings, no destroyed roads. A stark difference to the landscape to Lebanon.

There is no evenness in war, Rodger.

Going through the customs gate at the Charles de Gaulle Airport in Paris, the officer in the window points out that my connecting flight to LA doesn't leave for another three days.

Heaving a deep sigh, I reply sarcastically, "I died once on this journey. I can't be angry anymore."

She laughs, thinking it's a joke, and welcomes me to France.

Walking through the glass-domed terminals, I'm taken aback by everyone's ignorance to the fact that just a few hours away, children are dying under the rain of rocket fire. It's mind-blowing how easy it is to just flip the TV channel and stay in the comfort of our own bubbles. Inside, I just want to scream. With nowhere to go, I take a seat on a cold plastic chair and rest my head on my LV bag. Hugging my papyrus, I close my tired eyes for a second.

"Monsieur! Monsieur!" a spirited voice wakes me up. I notice a man in his 50s, in a uniform, leaning over me and tapping my shoulder.

"Sorry, I don't speak French," I say to him, wiping my sleepy eyes.

"Monsieur, it's the middle of the night. Did you miss your flight?" he asks kindly, with genuine concern in his voice.

"No. My flight doesn't leave for another three days. I have a connecting flight here from Jordan to Los Angeles."

"From Jordan, monsieur?"

"Yes, I escaped the war in Lebanon," I reply.

"Oh, *mon dieu*… I'm so sorry. It's a tragedy what is happening to those people. Are you hungry? *Un instant*." He smiles and leaves without waiting for my response, returning with a baguette sandwich and a bottle of water.

Another good omen, Rodger.

"*Voici*! I will check on you on my shifts. *Au revoir*!" the good Samaritan says before walking off.

With zero cash to my name, the free baguette tastes heavenly. I devour it. Having not eaten in days, the sandwich puts me in a food coma, as I slump over onto my bag once again, dead asleep.

In the early morning, I wake up to a gentle tap on my back. Still slumped over onto my LV bag, I sit up and see my papyrus being pointed at me by an older man dressed all in black.

"Sorry to wake you. This must be yours. It rolled away from you," he says as I get a glimpse of his kind eyes in the shadow of his hat and grey side-locks.

"Oh, thanks, I didn't even realize it fell," I reply to his bearded face, noticing he belongs to the long line of Jews boarding a flight to Tel Aviv right in front of me.

"This is an Egyptian papyrus, very valuable. Are you traveling from Egypt?" he asks while stroking his long, silver beard.

Hesitating for a second, if I should be honest with the man, I reply somberly, "No, sir. I just escaped the war in Lebanon."

His eyes go wide with a glint of sadness. He turns toward the other men in line and says something in Hebrew to them. They quickly start huddling around me, invading my space, as the word *Lebanon* echoes among them.

As the group, all in black clothing and hats, peers at me, he grasps my hand between his soft, squishy hands and says, "We have never forgotten to love our neighbors. The Torah commands us not to kill. We are people of peace. We are deeply sorry for what our government has done. Please, let us pray for you."

I look at his sorrowful eyes, astounded. As I nod to him silently, a solitary tear rolls down my cheek and they pray in unison. With my head bowed and my eyes closed, encircled by these beautiful Jews chanting and swaying, I hear a similarity to Abdul's Muslim morning prayers. They sound the same to me, songs of love for one God.

Can't make this shit up, Rodger.

I'm sitting here, basking in the irony of this moment, realizing that the same people who are now singing prayers for me are not the same Israelis who rained death from the Lebanese skies. People are not their governments, God is all religions, and in the end I still know nothing. As my devout grandmother once told me when I was questioning the origins of the Bible, "All that matters, my son, is that you are a believer."

My eyes slowly open as their prayers cease. Somehow, I feel lighter, as if a stone in my heart has been lifted. The kind men gather in a circle, whispering in Hebrew, before the old man with a silver beard comes forward, his hands outstretched.

"There are no coincidences. God put us on your path for a reason. Please accept this small gift from all of us." He takes my hand and puts a bundle of cash in it.

Stunned by their compassion and generosity, I say, with tears streaming down my face, "Thank you. I won't forget what you did for a stranger."

He taps me on the back and all the men wave goodbye, and he makes his way for the final boarding call on the flight to Tel Aviv.

Hours go by and I'm still sitting in the same slippery plastic airport seat, watching people arrive and leave all day, thinking to myself if this journey is what Rodger really had in mind for me.

Looking through the airport's glass ceiling up to the white clouds, I finally recognize my teacher's purposeful omission. The most arduous task of my journey is not filling my vessel but emptying it.

I get up and start walking through the terminal and find myself in a taxi heading toward Paris. Still in an introspective trance, I walk through the leafy streets of La Ville Lumière till nightfall.

Before making my way through the grassy colonnade toward the Eiffel Tower, I stop at a payphone and dial the number of the only person I want to hear from.

"Hello?" Her voice sends shivers down my spine.

"Aleyna, it's me," I say, having difficulty finding words.

"Where are you? Are you okay?" she screams down the phone with elation to hear me alive.

"I'm okay... made it to Paris... finally going home soon," I say in rasps, getting choked up by the sound of her sweet voice.

"I'm in Dusseldorf. I'll come to Paris tonight to see you, my love. I've been so worried about you. I miss you so much, Ashe." I can hear her pushing back the tears.

"Stay safe with your family, *hayete*. I must go home. I just can't take anymore." My voice shakes as I hear her crying. A switch goes off for me at this moment and I shut down. I've had enough of living in persistent fear and dread.

After a brief silence, she says, through the sobs piercing my heart, "My love for you is like the war, easy to begin and hard to end."

The call drops and I'm out of coins for the phone. Another omen?

I step away from the phone booth, wiping away the tears, wishing I'd said something meaningful, and pointlessly head toward the Eiffel Tower. As the Iron Lady starts flickering with her white metal stars, so bright in my eyes, I fall to the grassy ground and see again the rockets flying over Danny's chalet in Jounieh. I don't know if I am exhausted or drained, but I can barely stand. Kneeling on the ground, I see young lovers walking past, holding hands. I think of the last time I saw Aleyna, smiling at me over her shoulder, her golden hair windswept in the breeze of the waiting helicopter, with a glimmer of cedar trees behind her.

Now remembering, I, too, was in love before a storm of rockets washed away my elaborate dreams. I feel it here, like some memory I cannot place, like a grand love I forgot to have. I feel it like a mountain shaken by the mighty thunder. She filled my vessel with magic and wonder, before the hand of fate abruptly emptied it. This warm wonderful city that had brought me so much happiness became bleak and unrecognizable. All the laughter, the parties, the sunsets, the terrifying moments that I'd shared with my new friends rattling around my mind are inescapable.

I try to stop myself from thinking about all the cruelty that I've seen and all the beauty, the dreams and life that was lost.

The memories I have of Aleyna just don't seem real enough after this war. Yet, somehow, I know the shadow of her love will envelop all my days, the unknown will forever be... lost in Beirut.

ABOUT THE AUTHORS
ASHE & MAGDALENA STEVENS

Ashe and Magdalena Stevens are a dynamic author couple who call Los Angeles their home. With a diverse educational background that includes Theatre, Writing, Art History, and Medicine, their writing is imbued with a unique perspective that has captured the hearts and minds of readers worldwide.

Ashe and Magdalena are currently working on their highly anticipated second book, which promises to be as captivating and impactful as their first. When not writing, they enjoy spending time with their daughter and their furry friends, indulging in their love of reading, independent films, and exploring the world of art through frequent visits to galleries.

ACKNOWLEDGMENTS

We would like to extend our deepest gratitude to the marvelous editors Heather Sangster, Britt Collins and Tyrone Hodge for their guiding light and wisdom. We believe this story chose you and we are forever grateful.

We would also like to extend our sincere thanks to the wondrous cover designer Xavier Comas, the founder and director of Coverkitchen, for capturing the essence of *Lost in Beirut* with such clever artistry.

We need to recognize the superb website designer Kiersten Armstrong for creating an unforgettable space with beautiful imagery to accompany our words.

Finally, to our beloved daughter, Lucrezia Stevens: thank you for giving us the courage to spill the words onto paper and always inspiring us to do everything with love.

Made in the USA
Monee, IL
21 December 2023

50289403R00152